Father Nicastro has captured the authentic spirit of the popular devotion to Saint Gerard. More than mere nostalgia and certainly more profound than just ethnic heritage, he opens the treasure chest of Catholic and Italian patrimony. While immigrants in the New World clung tightly to their Old World traditions and customs, subsequent generations inherited a rich and invaluable gift from their immediate ancestors. This book shows that there has been and will always be a close relationship between an American parish (St. Lucy's, Newark, New Jersey) and an eighteenth-century saintly hero (St. Gerard Majella). Yet, the influence of this young man of God transcends time and space, and the feast in his honor is but a colorful way in which the Catholic faith and Italo-American culture not only overlap and intersect but where they also punctuate the landscape with love, devotion and hope in Divine Providence.

—Reverend Father Kenneth Brighenti, PhD
Vice Rector, Mount St. Mary Seminary (Emmitsburg, Maryland)
Co-Author of Catholicism for Dummies *and* Catholic Mass for Dummies
Eternal Word Television Network (EWTN) Co-Host of Web of Faith 2.0 *and*
Crash Course in Catholicism

The Feast of St. Gerard Maiella, C.Ss.R. *is a book that poignantly shows the importance and impact of a century-old Catholic and Italian devotion. Today, more than ever before, our contemporary society needs to hear and retell the story of faith that is Saint Gerard. While every immigrant has his or her own story why they came here and made this country their new home, Father Tom shows the relevance of this particular story about real faith and real devotion. Tradition is what is handed down to us, and the legacy of a person, Saint Gerard, and a place, St. Lucy's, is a journey not just into the past but also a road to a hopeful future. The author illumines the life and history of a Redemptorist saint whose humility and sanctity are as vital to all of us today as is his perennial intercession for pregnant mothers for ages to come. Here is something that brings back memories but also gives encouragement for today and tomorrow.*

—Reverend Father John Trigilio Jr., PhD, ThD
President, Confraternity of Catholic Clergy
Co-Author of Catholicism for Dummies *and* Catholicism Answer Book
EWTN Co-Host of Web of Faith *and* Council of Faith
Regular Guest Host on Catholic Answers Radio

In [this book], Father Thomas Domenick Nicastro, Associate Pastor of Saint Mary's Church in Nutley, New Jersey, produced a well-written and prodigiously researched and documented account of the Feast of Saint Gerard. The author recounts the history of the Feast from the birth of Saint Gerard Maiella, in Muro Lucano, Basilicata, to the Church of Saint Lucy in Newark. His insight is highlighted with anecdotal accounts of his grandmother, which enhance the account of this rich cultural treasure in the Italian American community.

—Cav. Gilda Rorro Baldassari, EdD
Honorary Vice Consul for Italy in Trenton, Emerita
Consular correspondent
Chair, New Jersey Italian and Italian American Heritage Commission

Father Tom Nicastro has been a loyal and faithful devotee of St. Gerard all his life. He has participated in the Feast and the Processions since he was old enough to walk. He has a complete grasp of the cultural, social and religious aspects of the Feast. Therefore, he is in the unique position to put his experiences on paper. He has done an admirable job of making the annual Feast of St. Gerard come alive for the reader.

—Reverend Monsignor Joseph J. Granato
Pastor Emeritus, St. Lucy's Church, Newark, New Jersey

A remarkable book—a verbal "pilgrimage" that combines sitting at your grandmother's knee with detailed research and interviews illuminating the St. Gerard Feast at St. Lucy's Church. This is a spiritual and personal journey— faith and history—the love story of the original First Warders and their beloved church and saint. It steps back in time, with emotional resonance, giving life to the Italian immigrants who settled in Newark.

—Sandra S. Lee, PhD, Professor, Seton Hall University; Author, Images of America: Italian Americans of Newark, Belleville, and Nutley.

THE FEAST OF
ST. GERARD MAIELLA
&-C.Ss.R.-&

A Century of Devotion at St. Lucy's, Newark, New Jersey

REVEREND THOMAS D. NICASTRO

THE
History
PRESS

Published by The History Press
Charleston, SC 29403
www.historypress.net

First published 2012

ISBN 978.1.60949.807.8

Library of Congress CIP data applied for.

Notice: The information in this book is true and complete to the best of our knowledge. It is offered without guarantee on the part of the author or The History Press. The author and The History Press disclaim all liability in connection with the use of this book.

I dedicate this book to the loving memory of my maternal grandparents, Anna (Maria Nicola) nee Liloia and Domenico Miano, parishioners of St. Lucy's Church and devotees of St. Gerard.
In loving memory of my paternal grandparents, Florence and Philip Nicastro.
In honor of my loving mother Filomena (Phyllis) and in loving memory of my father, Gaetano (Tom) Nicastro.
In honor of my sister Lisa and brother Domenick.
In memory of my Spiritual Director, Reverend Joseph F.X. Cevetello.
In honor of Monsignor Joseph Granato, Pastor Emeritus of St. Lucy's Church.
In memory of Reverend Joseph Nativo, Associate Pastor of St. Lucy's Church.
In memory of Reverend Domenico Barillá, C.Ss.R., former Rector of the International Shrine of St. Gerard, Materdomini, Italy (AV).
In memory of Deacon Louis Loffredo, Permanent Deacon of St. Lucy's Church and zealous devotee of St. Gerard.
In memory of Geta Spatola O'Connor, zealous devotee of St. Gerard.
A special dedication to my maternal grandmother, Anna (Maria Nicola) Miano, who first gave this beautiful devotion to me many years ago as a young boy.
Lastly, this work is dedicated to all the unsung, unmentioned devotees of St. Gerard's feast in "Newark's Little Italy, the Vanished First Ward," who year after year handed on this living, loving tradition and feast from October 16, 1899, to the present.

May Brother Gerard Maiella, C.Ss.R., Saint of Heaven and Earth, always intercede for all of you.

Contents

Foreword

Father Tom Nicastro's one-hundred-year history of the Feast of St. Gerard at St. Lucy's is a job well done.

He has documented through actual records and news reports the names, dates and places of all the elements involved in the design, development and execution of the feast.

He has cleared up for many of us the names of the personalities, the founders, the officers and the membership of the societies. I will be the first to admit that I derived very clear information about the early days of the feast from this book.

Father Tom has also explained the religious, devotional, cultural and financial aspects of this unique spiritual exercise.

He gives due credit to Father Gaetano Ruggiero for protecting the future financial stability of the parish by taking over complete control of the feast.

This book is a pleasure to read and also to refer to. It should be in everyone's library.

We owe a debt of gratitude to Father Tom Nicastro for his wonderful treatment of *The Feast of Saint Gerard Maiella, C.Ss.R.*

Reverend Monsignor Joseph J. Granato
Pastor Emeritus, St. Lucy Church

Acknowledgements

I t is with a deep sense of gratitude and appreciation that I give special acknowledgement and recognition to certain people who, without their guidance, assistance, time, talent, treasure, advice and support, I could not have completed this work on the history of the feast of our beloved saint, St. Gerard Maiella, C.Ss.R.

I owe a debt of gratitude to my family: to my mother, Phyllis; my deceased father, Gaetano, "Tom"; my sister Lisa; and brother Domenick for their love, support and encouragement over the years to complete this work.

To Mrs. Virginia Salerno, I am most grateful. She has graciously accepted to enter this work into the computer and has given most generously of her time, talent and treasure in typing the manuscript and making many revisions and changes. Over the last several years, she has been most generous and patient in working with me to be able to present this manuscript in its final form. May good St. Gerard abundantly bless her and answer all her prayers since this has been a real, genuine labor of love and devotion on her part. I am truly most grateful to her and her family.

To Mr. John Rendfrey, my childhood friend, I am most appreciative as well, for his gracious assistance and patience during my period of research in putting the story together and in collecting and assigning captions to all of the photographs collected for possible use in this book, photographs that follow the story line.

To Dr. Michael Credico, my close friend, who very graciously and diligently proofread the manuscript and offered valuable suggestions.

To Dr. Constance Ferrante for taking the time from her very busy schedule to proofread the manuscript and offer suggestions and valuable insights to the manuscript in its final form. Her doctoral thesis, "A Walk Through Time," was of great help in analyzing the feast of St. Gerard from an anthropological point of view.

To Michael Immerso, his work on the First Ward entitled *Newark's Little Italy: The Vanished First Ward* was of immense help in my research period and writing as well. The photos from his collection at the Newark Public Library were a precious source of pictorial memories of the history of the First Ward, the St. Gerard Feast and St. Lucy's Church. Michael, I am most grateful to you.

To my priest classmates and friends: Reverend Kenneth Brighenti, Vice Rector of Mount St. Mary's Seminary, Emmittsburg, Maryland; and Reverend John Trigilio, president of the Confraternity of Catholic Clergy, accomplished authors and frequent contributors to various series on EWTN. Your friendship is greatly appreciated.

To Mr. George Hawley, supervising librarian of the Charles F. Cummings New Jersey Information Center of the Newark Public Library, and the Newark Public Library staff for their gracious assistance, encouragement and support in many ways, especially with the usage of precious photos in the Immerso Collection of the "Old First Ward," your cooperation is greatly appreciated.

I wish to acknowledge and thank Monsignor Joseph Granato for all his time, concern, support and advice in proofreading the manuscript to make sure I got the facts down correctly. We thank you for all you have done and continue to do to build up not only St. Lucy's Church but also its greatest tradition, the annual Feast of St. Gerard.

The St. Gerard Plaza, which was constructed under your pastorate and guidance to mark the 100th anniversary of the Feast of St. Gerard, will stand as a lasting monument to our ancestors who built St. Lucy's and began the Feast of St. Gerard. The plaza will be a lasting reminder and memorial to the Italian immigrants who built up the "Old First Ward" and made it the thriving Little Italy it once was. Monsignor, thank you for allowing me the privilege of giving the St. Gerard novena each year.

To Father Luigi Zanotto, the present pastor of St. Lucy's, thank you for your kindness and generosity in allowing me to continue giving the St. Gerard novena each year, I am most grateful to you as well.

I wish to acknowledge the following people as well who have provided great support and inspiration in encouraging me to complete this work, a labor of love that needed to be recorded for posterity.

ACKNOWLEDGEMENTS

Most Reverend John J. Myers, Archbishop of Newark; Most Reverend Arthur J. Serratelli, Bishop of Paterson; Most Reverend Nicholas A. DiMarzio, Bishop of Brooklyn; Reverend Carl Hoegerl, C.Ss.R. archivist of the Redemptorist's New York Province; Reverend Monsignor Benjamin Piazza; Reverend Monsignor Ronald Marczewski; Reverend Dante DiGirolamo; Mr. and Mrs. Philip Nicastro; Dr. and Mrs. Michael Credico, Michael Credico Jr., Cindy Ann Credico, and the Credico family; Mr. and Mrs. Mario Socci; Raymond Salerno Jr.; Rosemary Seagriff; Cav. and Mrs. Joseph Coccia; Susan LaMorte; Edie Liguori; Lou Liguori; Bina Spatola; Gerald Spatola O'Connor; Pasquale Meola; Mr. and Mrs. Louis Garruto; Dr. and Mrs. Enio Callouri; the Honorable and Mrs. Joseph DiVincenzo; Rocco Ferrante Jr.; Mr. and Mrs. Gary Genuario; Gary Genuario Jr.; Mr. Michael Amante ; Bob Cascella, curator of the First Ward Museum; Anthony Pascucci; Dennis Tucci; Mr. and Mrs. Joseph DeBlasio; Mr. and Mrs. Walter Genuario; Dennis Genuario; Mr. & Mrs. Joseph Viscido; the Loffredo family; Lisa Manderichio; Steve Sefcik; Anthony Rosamilia; Mr. and Mrs. Louis Falconeri; Jerry DelTufo; Mr. and Mrs. Alan Genuario; Joseph Gonnella; Frank Panico; Theresa Colamedici; Mina Yannuzzi; Rosemarie Giannetta; Nicole D. Carbone; Andrzej Praszczyk; A.J. "Buddy" Fortunato, publisher of the *Italian Tribune News*; Marion Fortunato and Joan Alagna; Mr. and Mrs. Steve Adubato Sr.; Steve Adubato Jr.; Dr. Joseph Rosania and the Saint Gerard Novena Ladies; Anne Facciponte; Vincenza M. Farco; Jeanne Iuliani; Geraldine Miele; and Danielle Tangorra. In memoriam: Charles Cummings, Newark Public Library; Officer Rocco Andreotolla; Mrs. Seema Amante; Marian DelGaizo. If I have forgotten to acknowledge anyone, I ask your pardon.

Introduction

A s I embark upon what some might call the task of documenting the research I have done over the past several years concerning my devotion to the humble saint of Muro Lucano, namely Gerard Maiella or Majella as he is known in the United States, I want you to know that it is more a labor of love and devotion than anything else.

As I share my story in a reflective manner in order to express my family heritage and devotion to St. Gerard Maiella, I hope this work will contribute to a greater awareness of the devotion to St. Gerard and the historical significance of the "Old First Ward." Perhaps, as well, it will encourage a deeper understanding of the faith of the devotees and will promote a special dialogue among church historians, devotees and secular historians who will appreciate the impact that St. Gerard Maiella has had on so many lives in so many ways.

Ever since my earliest years, as far back as I could remember, this great saint, the unofficial patron of expectant mothers and their children, has captured my heart and soul as only he can. The very idea of writing down the collective thoughts and memories of this saint's devotees was conceived early on in my adolescent years. Oftentimes during those years, I found myself reading with great eagerness and interest the lives of the saints. Hagiography (the study of the lives of the saints) fascinated me as I yearned to know more and more about these heroes of God. In particular, I wanted to study the life of St. Gerard. Soon, I came to learn that he was known as the great wonderworker of the eighteenth century.

As I grew older, I began to realize that "the life of St. Gerard was not merely full of marvel, but is also rich in practical lessons."[1] My childhood experiences not only included this favorite pastime of reading the lives of the saints but also the joy of growing up in an Italian American family. I fondly recall those many family gatherings on Sunday afternoons with my maternal grandmother, Anna (Maria Nicola) Miano nee Liloia as the focus of our attention. It was there, over Sunday dinner, which was more like an Italian feast, that she shared her stories about growing up in Newark's "Little Italy." She was a woman of profound faith who came to America from the Old Country. Having grown up in an Italian Catholic family, devotion to the saints and love for her church was an important part of her daily life.

Those wonderful Sunday family get-togethers over flowed into the weekdays and weeknights as well, since my maternal grandmother lived with us. Many a time, she shared with me in her native dialect the stories of those early years in the "Old First Ward" of Newark with St. Lucy's Church at center stage.

Circa 1905, when she first came from Italy, her pastor was Father Joseph Perotti. My grandmother shared with me that he showed a genuine concern and love for his flock of Italian immigrants. His pastoral zeal consumed every hour of his day as he helped families get through the difficult periods in their lives. Most of all, she spoke of his holiness; everyone, she said, regarded him as a living saint. All Father Joseph Perotti had was a simple room for a rectory, if you could call it that, on Eighth Avenue, something the church didn't even own. When he died, his room was found to be completely bare.

Along with this story, she shared with us her frequently recited memories of the religious feasts celebrated each year from June, starting with the feast of St. Anthony, right through the summer and into the fall, with the feast of St. Michael

Anna (Maria Nicola) Miano (née Liloia), Father Tom Nicastro's maternal grandmother. *Courtesy of the archives of Reverend Thomas D. Nicastro Jr.*

Top: Domenico Miano, maternal grandfather of Father Tom Nicastro. *Courtesy of the archives of Reverend Thomas D. Nicastro Jr.*

Bottom: Wedding of Domenico and Anna (Maria Nicola) Miano, maternal grandparents of Father Tom Nicastro, October 1914 at St. Lucy's Church. *Courtesy of the archives of Reverend Thomas D. Nicastro Jr.*

in September and ending in a blaze of glory in October with the feast of St. Gerard on October 16.

As time marched on and the years flew by, she said, the feasts began to dwindle with the many changes in the neighborhood. The one feast that continued to grow each year was the ever-popular feast of St. Gerard, the unofficial patron of mothers, their children and the unborn.

All the feasts were marked with fervor and devotion, but this one saint captured the hearts of everyone. During his feast in October, especially on "his day," no one went to work. It was a tradition in my grandmother's family, even when she married, that her husband, Dominic, did not work on St. Gerard's feast day. She told me about the many beautiful customs and rituals people practiced during the feast and the processions that are unfortunately no longer continued today.

As you will see later on in this work, I will cover the history of this feast at the National Shrine of St. Gerard Maiella in the United States. Devotion to St. Gerard became one of the key elements in the history of this local ethnic church. This is evidenced by the fact that as early as the 1930s, baptismal certificates stated clearly that the church was known as St. Lucy's Church, Sanctuary of St. Gerard (printed in Italian).

What my grandmother and many other grandmothers who lived in the

17

"Old First Ward" clearly wanted to do was hand on the living tradition of this ever-growing devotion to St. Gerard.

In my own family, this devotion reaches back into the Liloia family, my maternal grandmother's maiden name, prior to her coming to America. For over 150 years, this devotion has been passed on from one generation to another in my family.

This living tradition spans the ocean and takes one back to a small town in southern Italy, the town of Teora. Teora is located next to the town of Caposele, where the famous Redemptorist Monastery and Shrine to St. Gerard—called Materdomini, "Mother of the Lord" in English—is located on the top of the mountain at Materdomini. It was there, in the little town of Teora, that the Liloia family made many a pilgrimage on foot to Materdomini, which houses the remains of this great saint.

My grandmother told me about the many trips her family made to the shrine, especially the last one they made before coming to America. They were sad because they did not know if they would ever return, but they took this devotion with them across the ocean to America.

Prior to the earthquake in southern Italy in 1982, there was a reminder of this devotion to St. Gerard erected in Teora. Cousins of mine (Joseph and Eva Liloia and family) donated two statues for the two outside niches of the town's church (Chiesa Madre, meaning "Mother Church").

Exterior of the Old Church following the renovation that took place after the 1980 earthquake in Materdomini, Italy. *Courtesy of the archives of Reverend Thomas D. Nicastro Jr.*

Father Tom Nicastro kneeling in front of St. Gerard's Tomb in the Old Church at Materdomini, the International Shrine of St. Gerard in Avellino, Italy. *Courtesy of the archives of Reverend Thomas D. Nicastro Jr.*

One statue was St. Gerard; the other was San Nicola, the patron of the Teoresi. The statues were erected in honor and memory of my cousin's parents, members of the Liloia family.

And so, as you can see, this beautiful devotion has spanned the ocean and taken root in the Italian colony in Newark, New Jersey, where I have my family roots in a church that has played a vital role in my family's life; that is where my maternal grandparents were married in October 1914 and where my mother was baptized in the 1930s.

What we are celebrating is over one hundred years of faith and devotion to St. Gerard at St. Lucy's. This celebration is not just one family's devotion but also many families who, over the past one hundred years, have walked through those hallowed doors of St. Lucy's Church. This includes anyone who has ever prayed to or invoked St. Gerard in need, not just for the needs of motherhood but also for many other problems that weigh down one's soul in this world of ours.

Yes, all those who have participated in the religious devotions at the National Shrine love St. Gerard in a very special way, but he is loved all over the world as well. Brother Gerard of Muro Lucano and Caposele is now St. Gerard of heaven and earth.

You may be wondering how I received the inspiration for this book on the history of the first one hundred years of the Feast of St. Gerard. Anyone who grew up or descended from Italian immigrants from Newark's "Old First Ward" will understand that this venerable feast was our grandparents' treasure, in particular our Italian grandmothers' treasure, which was passed down to us and has become our heritage. It is the living, loving tradition of the Feast of St. Gerard handed on to us. It has become our heritage and their legacy. It also is Angelo Pirofalo's great-grandson's treasure that he received from his grandmother. Originally, the words "My grandmother's treasure has become my heritage" were the words of his great-grandson. Let me explain. Upon leaving the Pirofalo family home one day, Brother Gerard dropped his handkerchief. When Angelo's daughter brought it to him as he was leaving, he said to her, "Keep it. Perhaps one day it may be useful to you." And so began a tradition which started with these words of great St. Gerard and his handkerchief.

Upon leaving the home of Angelo Pirofalo and his family, Gerard dropped his handkerchief and left them a precious treasure, a keepsake that would forever and for all times and places become his spiritual trademark, so to speak—what I would call "heaven's handkerchief."

In his work on the life of St. Gerard, Father Dilgskron writes, "With great respect and with special jealously was this relic preserved ever afterwards, until later her heirs cut it into small pieces in order to satisfy the wishes of the friends and admirers of the servant of God."[2] Father Carr (a biographer of St. Gerard) elaborates upon his story about the handkerchief with the words of the witness who recorded this fact, an heir of Angelo Pirofalo's daughter. Actually it was his great-grandson, the grandson of his daughter. Here's what he said: "My grandmother zealously preserved this miraculous handkerchief. Eventually it became my heritage, but now I have but a shred of it, as the rest has been cut up into small pieces for his clients."[3]

Interestingly, Carr then concludes the handkerchief story by saying, "Ever since, Gerard Majella has been busy the world over shepherding thousands of little ones to their mother's first caress and hovering like an angel of light and gladness round thousands of cradles. So closely has he identified himself with the relief of this particular sort of suffering that today there is a movement afoot to have him constituted patron of expectant mothers."[4]

Recently I had a great opportunity to return again to the sacred place and space where this all began. I returned to the land of my ancestors, the birthplace of my Italian grandparents, to reconnect with my grandmother's treasure—the heritage and devotion she passed on to me, a heritage and devotion she received from her parents and grandparents. I went to the same sacred place where she often prayed as a child in Italy, at the Shrine of St. Gerard at Materdomini. It was there that I went to the primary source and the heart of the matter. I went and knelt at the tomb of my childhood friend, Brother Gerardo Maiella.

As I knelt there in prayer, my mind drifted back in time. Memories began to flood my mind, memories of my childhood and teenage years when I embraced the heritage, culture and tradition that was handed on to me from my maternal grandmother. I also have vivid recollections of visiting with the late Father Barillá, the former rector of the International Shrine of St. Gerard. I will never forget what he said to me when he asked about the history of my devotion and how I received it. He said, *"Tu sei cresciuto nel mondo Gerardino!"*—"You were born into the Gerardian world!" I thought about the beliefs and customs that were passed on to me, the heritage of my Italian roots from past generations and the traditions of this great feast in honor St. Gerard.

As I pondered Father Barillá's words, I felt I was given a mandate to promote, protect and nurture this great treasure that was placed in my hands so many years ago as a child. I believe I was called to pass on these customs, traditions and beliefs.

Come and see; here is how it all began!

It was in Materdomini, a subsection of Caposele, that the first immigrants traversed the ocean so many years ago and settled here in Nevarca, Newark's "Old First Ward." It was on October 16, 1899, that St. Lucy's greatest tradition was born, the beautiful feast of St. Gerard. St. Lucy's Church and this beautiful feast would be forever linked. One cannot say enough about the role of St. Gerard and his impact on the Italians of Newark and St. Lucy's Church.

Many would agree that it is a beautiful love story between heaven and earth, between an Italian saint and the devoted faithful of Newark's "Old First Ward."

The feast has evolved over the years. The first fifty years were very ethnic in nature. The second fifty years saw an emphasis on a much larger group of devotees focusing on St. Gerard as patron of mothers, babies and the unborn. Our beautiful feast is a clear and definite link to the past—of what once was. If it dies out, the connection is gone. The feast, in some ways, is still like it was fifty years ago. St. Lucy's Church has always remained constant, a spiritual home for many, a refuge of peace, serenity, tradition, devotion and custom. This feast perpetuates itself with new believers who walk in procession from infancy.

St. Gerard was and is important to all immigrants and all people of different nationalities. He worked and lived and performed miracles for the people. Brother Gerard was truly "the saint of the people." He never refused help to those who came to him in need. He was always praying for them, guiding them, writing letters to them and performing miracles to meet the real needs of people.

At the conclusion of my work, there will be a detailed account of a remarkable woman who lived a simple lifestyle and yet was considered by many to be "heroic in virtue" and a "living saint." We will leave that for the Official Church to decide. Mary Grace Bellotti was a homemaker and midwife who exemplified "holiness in daily living." She is a beautiful example of a twentieth-century woman who followed the saints and who may very well one day be declared a saint herself. Her fascinating, compelling life story and struggle is about one layperson's journey with Saint Gerard, whom she invoked as her special patron when delivering babies as a midwife. She lived during the first half of the twentieth century in New Jersey. When you finish her story, you will read about those who actually knew her and give testimony to her "holy life."

Today as we recall and celebrate St. Gerard's holy life, we are called upon to pass on this treasure that we have all received from our parents and grandparents: the heritage, customs and traditions given to them. I invite you to instill in your children and grandchildren the treasures that you have received. You must instill in the next generation the great love and trust we have for this eighteenth-century wonderworker that we call our saint and friend. Yes, not only did Angelo Pirofalo's great-grandson receive a treasure from his grandmother when she passed on to him what was left of St. Gerard's original handkerchief, but we also have received a treasure from our grandparents and parents, our grandmothers, that being a living faith and devotion to great St. Gerard. We all need a place to celebrate our treasure, our customs and our devotion, a place where we can go where everything is the same as it was for our ancestors. That sacred place and space is St. Lucy's. St. Lucy's is our spiritual home, just as it was the spiritual home of our parents, grandparents and great-grandparents since 1891. It is here for the last 113 years that St. Gerard has his home forever linked with St. Lucy's Church. It has been said that "home is where the heart is." How true! The heart of your faith and devotion is here. Some have said, "You can never return home," or "It's just never the same;

St. Gerard in Heavenly Glory. Mural in St. Gerard's Chapel at the National Shrine. *Courtesy of the archives of the Museum of the "Old First Ward" of Newark, Curator, Mr. Bob Cascella.*

everything is changed." However, that is not true with St. Lucy's. It is here that you truly can go back home.

There is a real sense of peace, serenity and security there that you find no where else. The feast still celebrates many beautiful customs, some of which remain constant. What was said in the book about the "Old First Ward" is true. "The Church in turn provides the unbroken link with the past, with the vanished neighborhood. Only the church remains, timeless and changeless. And within the confines of the church, as one recognizes a familiar face, albeit age worn and wizened, it is easy for a moment to let the intervening years to fade from memory and to imagine the old neighborhood still thriving and alive outside the church doors."[5]

When you look to the church here, you think of it as St. Lucy's family. The priests here are the spiritual fathers of this family. They have shown and continue to show love for their family, the parishioners. They bring that love to the community, the parish. They are the spiritual leaders. They have become part of your families. Monsignor Joseph Granato has been there for over fifty-five years. As Lou Garruto, a coordinator of the feast, describes it, Monsignor Granato and the other priests have been with you in "good times and sad times...There isn't anything they wouldn't do for you." Monsignor Granato has often spoken about the importance of protecting and guiding our customs and traditions and this beautiful devotion to St. Gerard.

Our beautiful St. Gerard Plaza, constructed under his direction, recalls and remembers our ancestors who started St. Lucy's greatest tradition, the Feast of St. Gerard. It is a vivid reminder of this once great neighborhood. The legacy can be connected to the hopes and dreams of those gone before us. We should not forget our ancestors, our loved ones and all they did. New beginnings should not be devoid of our treasured past. The feast helps to perpetuate what we once had. The church and this feast is the one last bastion of hope, the link to the glorious past of the once thriving "Old First Ward" of Newark.

The St. Gerard Plaza is a symbol, too, of renewed hope that a new day is dawning. You might say, what can we do to carry on the traditions and customs and secure the legacy?

The following are what we should do:

Continue the tradition of the novena.

Say the prayers to St. Gerard.

Distribute the St. Gerard handkerchief.

Light your candles.

Make your vows.

Spread devotion to St. Gerard.

Walk in procession with the different generations.

Make a collection.

Pin your cape.

Support the Church generously.

Pray with great faith and hope.

Continue the time-honored tradition of not working on St. Gerard's feast day and walk in the procession with your family and attend the Feast Day Mass.

Remember that we are part of an unbroken chain, a link to what took place in the eighteenth century. How many people still follow the tradition of Alessandro Piccolo, the watchmaker from Muro Lucano? Alessandro called his son Gerardo while he was still in his mother's womb. What about the importance of naming our children after him in thanksgiving? If we do all of these things, we will carry on the customs and traditions and secure the legacy of this church and this feast for future generations. All of these things combined make the Feast of St. Gerard a sacred and timeless ritual of faith and devotion.

My dear devotees, as you stand before St. Gerard and light your candle and whisper your prayer, plead your cause, express your need or ask for your special grace and favor, remember that you are a part of an unbroken chain, a link to your ancestors who so often stood before him in the flesh, begging for his heavenly aid. Remember that he will not forget you. He is our saint, our friend and helper who now stands before Almighty God, interceding as he always did on our behalf.

When you touch the hem of his Redemptorist habit and spiritually connect with him and your ancestors, step back in time, even just for a moment, in the passages of your mind, embrace your grandparents' treasure, which became your heritage and mine, not so much his handkerchief but the traditions and customs they passed on to you and me.

Close your eyes for a moment and feel your ancestors' presence, visualize St. Gerard coming to your house in the "Old First Ward," listen to the music, embrace them, walk again with them in procession and then return to the church and to the feast outside. Reconnect with old friends and familiar faces, smell the aroma of the food, laugh, cry and pray. Walk again inside this sacred place, and experience the solitude and peace as you kneel before the tabernacle. Talk to Christ, truly present there, as St. Gerard did. When you leave to go back outside to the feast and walk on what once was old Sheffield Street, recall years gone by and imagine the old neighborhood alive and thriving once again. When you finally take leave and go back to your new home, away from the embrace of Newark's "Old First Ward," you will agree, I'm sure, that this day's experience and this year's feast was a real homecoming. Then you will know you were truly back home again at this sacred place where we once so long ago received our grandmother's treasure, a treasure that became your heritage and mine. Then one can say St. Lucy's Church and the Feast of St. Gerard gives you the warmth of a home, your real home, a spiritual one. Yes, this is the home of our ancestors in the faith. Who could dare say you can never really return home again?

I want to thank Monsignor Joseph Granato, pastor emeritus, the father of this family in faith for over fifty years, for this great and awesome privilege to share with each of you the Fioretti di San Gerardo, the little flowers and the pearls of wisdom of St. Gerard, one of the rarest and brightest stars

Father Tom Nicastro in St. Mary's Church, Ridgefield, CT, near an image of St. Gerard prior to St. Gerard Mass. *Courtesy of the archives of Reverend Thomas D. Nicastro Jr.*

in heaven, one of the great saints in the "Cloud of Witnesses" in heavenly glory. If this heartfelt work of love and devotion draws you, the reader, closer to Almighty God and great St. Gerard, then the author begs a brief prayer in return.

Go now and walk outside the church doors and recapture, even for a brief shining moment, the old neighborhood thriving once more and celebrate the Feast of St. Gerard, St. Lucy's greatest tradition and our great heritage. Our grandmothers' treasure!

God Bless You!
Viva San Gerardo Maiella!
April 6, 2011, the birthday of Great St. Gerard

Chapter 1

The Early Years:

An Italian Saint and the Devoted Faithful of Newark's "Old First Ward"

The story I am about to share with you is a timeless love story between an Italian saint and his devoted faithful of Newark's "Old First Ward." Sometimes in our lives, the most treasured and special things are the most difficult things to put into writing because words, at times, can be so inadequate to describe the joy that they bring to us—in this case, the joy that a saint of God brings to our hearts and souls.

The life of every saint of God is truly a loving discourse that weds heaven and earth. There exists a spiritual bond between a saint and his or her devoted faithful. Angela Bonilla, in the January 26, 1997 edition of *Our Sunday Visitor*, said in her article "Lovers of God and their Land" that "great Saints were not only lovers of God, but also lovers of their land and their people." How true these words are, especially in the relationship between St. Gerard and those of Italian descent. Such is the case with my lifelong devotion to St. Gerard, a devotion that is very special in my family's life for over 150 years and, so too, in the lives and families of many Italian immigrants who settled in Newark's "Old First Ward."

This story is a celebration of over one hundred years of faith and devotion to our beloved St. Gerard Maiella.

The October 14, 1997 edition of the *Newark Star Ledger* said, "Each October countless scattered Italian Americans from all over the United States come on pilgrimage and make a joyful return to the 'old neighborhood' for the annual feast of St. Gerard at St. Lucy's Church in Newark, N.J." They come because they wish to express their outward devotion to a gentle saint who has touched their lives and their ancestor's lives in numerous ways.

Even though the old neighborhood is not thriving as it once did, the Feast of St. Gerard and St. Lucy's Church provide devotees with a real sense of belonging and a sacred place to reenact the traditions, sights and sounds of yesteryear. For over one hundred years, the celebration of this venerable feast has been the spiritual catalyst to bring back to life the "Old First Ward," the "Italian Brigadoon."

This unbelievable story is told by each member of the various generations still coming together to share their families' stories intertwined in the unique and rich history of this special place. You can see it in their eyes, in their faces and in their hearts as they recount the memories and miracles of their parents and grandparents still present to them in the hallowed walls of the magnificent church that we call Santa Lucia—St. Lucy's, "the Italian cathedral."

It is interesting to note that many who return each year are either those who grew up with this tradition or relatives of theirs. In any case, those who come to venerate St. Gerard are descendants of villagers who actually lived and worked beside St. Gerard in the old country. Today, there are numerous devotees of various ethnic backgrounds who also come and venerate this gentle Italian saint, a tailor's son from Muro Lucano.

Although our story about St. Gerard begins on April 6, 1726, with his birth, the celebration really begins over one hundred years ago in the southern province of Avellino.

Join me now on a voyage across the ocean to Southern Italy in the latter part of the nineteenth century. The region of this part of Italy is known as Campania. Unfortunately, at that time, the region was afflicted with a series of financial setbacks and misfortunes that drove many to leave behind the land they so loved. A great many of these simple hardworking people were our ancestors, simple peasant farmers, *contadine* from the small towns and villages of Campania.

About the time of the unification of Italy, southern Italians began arriving and settling in Newark, or Nevarca, as it is still called by those who live in towns like Caposele, Teora, Lioni and others in the province of Avellino.

As a result of this mass migration, one particular southern town in the Campania region has played an important role in our spiritual lives for the last one hundred years and more. The town is Caposele; it is an agricultural center of the province Avellino. This quaint little town is located at the head

Oldest known photograph of St. Gerard Statue in procession, 1906. *Courtesy of the Spatola family archives.*

of the Sele River. Hence, it received its name Caposele, meaning head of the Sele River.

It is in a "geographically strategic area that separates the Sele Valley, leading to the Turrenian Sea, from the Ofanto Valley leading to the Adriatic."[6] It is here we find the famous springs of Caposele, with their refreshing water that collected and channeled into what is the longest of the aqueducts, the *Acudotto Pugliese.*[7]

In spite of the enormous quantity of water in this region, the economic situation at that time (late 1880s) coupled with natural disasters forced these hardworking peasants to seek a better life. They heard about America and a place called Nevarca, and so they came to settle and build. They brought with them their language, culture, traditions and religious beliefs, especially their Old World expressions and devotions to the saint of their *paese* (their town or village).

With hope in their hearts and a deep trust in God and his saints, they packed the few belongings and earthly possessions they owned and set out for America. Immigrants from Caposele, along with the neighboring towns of Teora, Calabritto, Lioni, Maddaloni, Castelgrande, San Fele, Ariano Irpino, Monocalzati and other places, began to settle in Newark's Little Italy. It was the first and largest Italian colony in the state of New Jersey. "Newark thus became one of the first cities in the country outside of New York with a large Italian immigrant community. At the turn of the century, its Italian population ranked fifth in size nationwide, exceeded only by New York, Philadelphia, Chicago and Boston. Newark's most densely populated 'Little Italy' was concentrated in the First Ward."[8] Prior to being called the First Ward, that section was originally the Fifteenth Ward. As the city grew, the wards were switched around, and districts changed around 1915.

"The U.S. Census of 1870 recorded 29 Italians in Newark and 257 throughout the state. The first large stream poured into Newark between 1870 and 1900, 10,000 Italians made their homes in Newark."[9]

In response to the great influx of Italian immigrants to the area, a decision was made by the then Diocese of Newark to establish a national parish within the boundaries of the Old Fifteenth Ward (later First Ward) to meet the pastoral needs of the Italian colony that was ever growing. This decision was made with the prime responsibility of caring for the souls of these immigrants.

Therefore, on September 20, 1891, St. Lucy's Catholic Church was incorporated, and the cornerstone was laid on December 13 of that same year. The role that St. Lucy's was to play in the lives of these immigrants

The Early Years

Italian immigrants arrive at Ellis Island, early 1900. *Courtesy of the Newark Public Library M. Immerso Collection of the "Old First Ward," Charles F. Cummings New Jersey Information Center, Mr. George Hawley, Supervising Librarian.*

from Southern Italy was in direct relation to the key role the Catholic Church played in the southern region of Campania. "Village based solidarity (campanilismo) was measured by proximity to the bell tower (campanile) of the local church."[10] So, too, in the United States, the immigrants consciously sought to settle themselves as close as possible to the church, which became literally the center of their lives. Along with this, they brought the customs and devotions from their paese in Italy and tried as best as possible to recreate the demonstrative expression of their faith as they had practiced in the old country. Most especially, this was expressed when they celebrated the feast day of the saint of their town in Italy, their heavenly protector. As each group of immigrants settled into the "Old First Ward," they sent for a statue of their patron from their town in Italy. Gradually, St. Lucy's became a permanent home for each of these statues.

Prior to the unification of Italy and even after embarking to the New World, Italians did not think of themselves, at first, as Italian; they regarded themselves as Caposelesi, Teoresi, Calabrittani, San Felese, etc. Gradually,

Rear view of a typical house in the "Old First Ward." *Courtesy of the Newark Public Library M. Immerso Collection of the "Old First Ward," Charles F. Cummings New Jersey Information Center, Mr. George Hawley, Supervising Librarian.*

the church was transforming them into Italian Americans, with the church becoming the central figure in their social lives.

The history of the Feast of St. Gerard goes hand in hand with the history of St. Lucy's parish. The years between 1891 and 1897 were administered to by various priests, but it wasn't until 1897 that St. Lucy's saw the coming of a permanent shepherd who would guide the parish during those crucial years of its early development. In 1897, Father Joseph Perotti, born in northern Italy, arrived at St. Lucy's after serving for a short period in New York and Boston. When he arrived, this saintly priest found his flock struggling in poverty and debt, to say the least. Two years after his arrival as the new administrator, he became St. Lucy's first pastor in 1899.

This was a very important year in the spiritual life of the parishioners of St. Lucy's for more than one reason. First and foremost, they received their first pastor, the saintly priest who had worked among them for the last two years. Secondly, the parish, under the spiritual guidance of Father Joseph Perotti, saw the beginning of the greatest feast ever to be held at St. Lucy's, the Feast of St. Gerard Maiella. "From that time forward, St. Lucy's Church and St. Gerard Maiella would become forever linked."[11]

As you will see, the role of each of St. Lucy's pastors (three of them to date) goes hand in hand with significant events connected with the Feast of St. Gerard over a period of one hundred years from 1899 to 1999.

In his first years, Father Perotti thrust himself into establishing a school to educate the Italian children of his parish. He also sought the assistance of Mother Cabrini, who was already establishing a school at Mount Carmel Church in Newark's ironbound section. The missionary daughters of Mother Frances Xavier Cabrini came to St. Lucy's in 1902. Later the school project was to be continued by the Sisters of St. John the Baptist.

Father Joseph Perotti, the first pastor of St. Lucy's, poses for a photo. Circa early twentieth century. *Courtesy of the archives of Reverend Thomas D. Nicastro Jr.*

In the early years of the twentieth century, the church suffered a setback. There was a fire in the old wooden church. Thank God it was contained and did not destroy the church completely. Because the parish was growing in leaps and bounds, the congregation was quickly outgrowing the old wooden church built in 1892.

From the very beginning, the priests of St. Lucy's were devoted to their flock of Italian immigrants. The priests, being Italian themselves, understood the people's devotion to the saints. They understood, as well, their external demonstration of expressing their customs and rituals connected with the celebration of a saint's feast day. And yes, at St. Lucy's there were many feasts to be celebrated. Most certainly by this time the Catholic Church was a powerful influence in the poor immigrants' lives. They were guided by faith, custom and ritual.

The first signs of devotion to Beato Gerardo, or Blessed Gerard, as he was affectionately called by his early devotees, are lost in the humble beginnings of the Italian colony in Newark's "Old Fifteenth Ward."

There are different oral traditions circulating among different groups as to who may have originated the humble beginnings of this devotion in America and, later on, the feast to honor Blessed Gerard, as he was known prior to canonization.

Oral tradition tells us that the Caposelesi immigrants brought this devotion with them from the shrine at Materdomini. A celebration in his honor was well underway in the Campania and Basilicata regions of Southern Italy, as well, as in other parts of the world.

The fervent devotion to Brother Gerard Maiella began in Newark probably in the 1880s, but a celebration of a feast in his honor began in a formal way on October 16, 1899. And thus, "St. Lucy's greatest tradition was born," as noted in the 1999 documentary for the 100th anniversary of the feast, entitled *A Walk Through Time*. It is interesting to note that this tradition began only a few short years after Brother Gerard was beatified in January 1893. The feast in his honor was initiated five years before he was canonized a saint on December 11, 1904. The origin of the feast was verified by the news media in 1929. On October 16, 1929, the *Newark News* stated that "the festivities are arranged by immigrants from a small village of Caposele, Italy. This year's celebration marked its thirtieth anniversary." Hence the beginning of the feast on October 16, 1899.

I believe that we should take the collective experience of these immigrants who came together as a unified group and expressed this devotion to Blessed Gerard. They manifested this by carrying a picture frame of him, or as they called it in Italian, a *quadro*. A large picture frame of Blessed Gerard was carried through the streets of the Fifteenth Ward. At the time, a modest monetary collection was taken up among his faithful devotees.

The Early Years

It is important for us, I believe, to understand the mindset of these immigrants as they struggled to assimilate into their new environment. "Religion, as a vehicle by which the immigrants were able to continue their beliefs, provided a comfortable liaison between Europe and the United States. In essence, religious beliefs and their differing modes of expression provided continuity to the community, especially to the immigrants."[12]

As we continue with our story, you will see how customs and traditions will be passed down from one generation to another. The first of these was the walking in procession and the pinning of the monetary donation first on the picture frame and then later on the habit of St. Gerard's statue.

Due to the rapid growth in devotion to Blessed Gerard Maiella, it was decided among the members of the Caposelesi colony to write to the shrine of St. Gerard in Materdomini to request that a statue be cast and sent to America. Unfortunately, to the best of our knowledge, there is no existing letter or documentation today in the Redemptorist archives at the Shrine of Materdomini or at St. Lucy's Church requesting such a statue.

There is an amusing story that explains how the venerable statue arrived here in America in the autumn of 1900. The arrival of the statue from Italy was an important event not only in the history of the feast but also in the life of St. Lucy's Parish and the lives of its Italian immigrant parishioners. The month was October, the year 1900. It was a brisk autumn day when Gerardo Spatola Sr., a livery stable operator and funeral director, set out for the docks of New York harbor. Along with him were members of the Caposelesi community. Little did one of the men realize that his wife would give birth the very day the statue was picked up. Raffaele Tubello, along with Gerardo Spatola and others, hitched up a horse and carriage and set out on what would become an interesting, comical venture. Geta Spatola O'Connor, the granddaughter of Gerardino, put it well when she spoke of this story.

The amusing story that unfolded that day still brings a smile to the faces of his devotees...they were hampered with the language barrier, and they were excitedly explaining to the pier officials they came to pick up Gerardo Maiella. After a lot of confusion, the harbormaster returned and said, "We can't seem to find a Gerardo Maiella on the passenger list." With that they had to go through the records, and they finally understood it was a statue. They sent them to the cargo dock; I believe it was the very same statue. He has taken on a life of His own...[13]

The statue is housed in a beautifully wrought high domed, marbleized sanctuary chapel built in 1935 by the San Gerardo Maiella Society." There was another happy ending to this story. The very day they arrived at the docks on October 12, 1900, Raffaele Tubello's wife gave birth to a baby girl named Jennie. Jennie often boasted that she was born the same day the statue was picked up and that she was as old as the venerable statue of St. Gerard.

Early on we have examples of the statue of our saint going out in procession. The newspapers, in particular, the *Newark Advertiser* of October 17, 1901, reported that after the masses were said, there was a parade in which thousands of people marched.

Portrait of Gerardo Spatola Sr. *Courtesy of the Spatola family archives.*

From the very beginning, we see evidence of immigrant devotees pinning money on the black habit of the statue. This was their expression of asking for a favor or giving thanks to the saint who interceded for them before the throne of God. Some articles from the newspaper reported that twelve men carried the statue and six men carried the canopy over his head.

As the feast grew each year, so too did new traditions. From the very beginning, music, especially a band for the procession with the saint, was an integral part of the annual celebration. As early as 1903, the band is specifically mentioned in the newspaper (*Newark Evening News*, October 16, 1903). There probably was a band that played in 1899, but the feast and the band are not mentioned in the news that year. The *Newark Advertiser* of October 18, 1904 reported a triple band concert given by F. Campione, A. Attanasio and C.G. Fulcoli. There were many selections from operas to please music lovers of the day. The *Newark Advertiser* of October 17, 1904 mentions "a large orchestra stand decorated in white and gold was built on the right side of the church. Present for the evening concert was sixty musicians and a 110 piece orchestra for the last evening of the feast."

1904 was a very significant year in the feast's history. Interestingly, the newspapers of the day were reporting on the feast and referring to him as

Members of the St. Gerard Committee and devotees pose for picture in the procession with statue of St. Gerard. *Courtesy of the Newark Public Library M. Immerso Collection of the "Old First Ward," Charles F. Cummings New Jersey Information Center, Mr. George Hawley, Supervising Librarian.*

Oldest known photograph of the St. Gerard Procession from 1906. Constable on right is Ottone Genuario, the grandfather of Gary Genuario Sr., a current member of the St. Lucy's Men's Choir. *Courtesy of the Spatola family archives.*

One of three bands that played music for the Feast of St. Gerard and other feasts at St. Lucy's. *Courtesy of the Newark Public Library M. Immerso Collection of the "Old First Ward," Charles F. Cummings New Jersey Information Center, Mr. George Hawley, Supervising Librarian.*

St. Gerard. Even the newspaper article of October 1904 referred to him as St. Gerard. However, the official declaration did not come until two months later, on December 11, 1904, when Pope Pius X declared him a saint, thus "confirming the remarkable life of this blessed man."[14] It was on that eventful day that the name Gerardo Maiella, a Redemptorist brother of Muro Lucano and Materdomini (Caposele), was inscribed in the catalogue of saints.

In October 1904, the Newark newspapers reported that the feast was organized by a group of Caposelesi men lead by Gerardo Spatola Sr. This would be part of a long history of members of the Spatola family actively participating in the feast of St. Gerard since its inception in 1899. One hundred years of tradition would be passed on beginning with Gerardo Spatola Sr., then to Gerardo J. Spatola, who handed this on to his daughters, Bina Spatola and Geta Spatola O'Connor, who in turn passed the devotion on to her son Gerald Spatola O'Connor.

In January 1905, there appeared in the weekly Italian newspaper *L'Ora* an article that was printed in a book recently published for the 100th anniversary of the canonization of St. Gerard in 2004. The book reprints the newspaper article that appeared in the St. Gerard magazine in Italian from 1905 (*St. Gerard Maiella* 4, no. 10 [May 2, 1905]: 176).

Here below is an English translation of what the newspaper article stated concerning the canonization of St. Gerard on December 11, 1904. Interestingly, it mentions what took place at St. Lucy's Church and whom the key figures were who organized and ran the celebration in honor of St. Gerard's canonization. The newspaper article states that the father of Jerry

The Early Years

Gerardo Spatola and members of the St. Gerard committee, circa 1905. *Courtesy of the Newark Public Library M. Immerso Collection of the "Old First Ward," Charles F. Cummings New Jersey Information Center, Mr. George Hawley, Supervising Librarian.*

Spatola and the grandfather of Geta Spatola O'Connor was in charge of the feast.

Newark—Last Sunday, in the Church of Saint Lucy, a solemn feast was held in honor of Saint Gerardo Maiella, who was sanctified in Saint Peters, Rome, Italy on the same day.

The Caposelesi residing here, who are so devoted to their glorious Saint, did not omit a thing in the preparation of an unexpected and pompous feast. In fact, the Church celebrated a Solemn Mass with the philharmonic of brothers Brizzi, and an eloquent panegyric, recited by Reverend Father Romanelli of Orange. He praised highly the life of the Saint with words that awoke in the hearts of all a deep admiration for the glorious protector of the Caposelesi.

The music of Cav. Fulcioli of Brooklyn, fighting the austerity of the times with his harmonious symphonic marches, kept the 15th quarter happy all day long.

There were battery of gunfire and all turned out well, thanks to the cooperation of the Caposelesi committee which was composed of the following

39

THE FEAST OF SAINT GERARD MAIELLA, C.Ss.R.

A classic view of the procession with banner of St. Gerard and members of the Gerardines, many young people and children in background. Banner with words "S. Gerardo, October 1924." *Courtesy of the Newark Public Library M. Immerso Collection of the "Old First Ward," Charles F. Cummings, New Jersey Information Center, Mr. George Hawley, Supervising Librarian.*

persons: G. Ilaria, President, L. Zarra, Treasurer, G. Caruso, Secretary, R. Rosania, F. Rosania, P. Masi, S. Iannuzzi, G. Capra and at the head of the feast of the 16th October, Mr. Gerardo Spatola, who together with the committee, will prepare next October an even greater feast than the preceding years.

After St. Gerard was canonized a saint in 1904, Father Joseph Perotti saw that the feast of St. Gerard at St. Lucy's was growing and taking on great importance in the life of the parish, and so he decided he would write a letter to the rector of the sanctuary at Materdomini where the International Shrine of St. Gerard was located in Southern Italy. Unfortunately, I have not been able to locate the letter he wrote; however, by Divine Providence, I came across a fascinating letter that was written in 1908 by the rector of the Shrine at Materdomini to Father Joseph Perotti, the first pastor of St. Lucy's. After translating the letter, I was not completely satisfied with the translation, so I showed the letter to Dr. Enio Callouri and asked for his expertise since he speaks Italian so well.

The Early Years

After reading the translation, I solved another mystery, something that had been bothering me for a long time. Where did the relic of St. Gerard come from, and who requested it? When did it arrive at St. Lucy's? Let's take a look at the letter written on April 22, 1908, a letter written to Father Joseph Perotti, pastor of St. Lucy's prior to him being named a monsignor.

It reads as follows:

Materdomini 22/4/1908
Most Reverend Pastor,
  Some time ago, I sent you reliquary of our Thaumaturgus, our wonderworker, St. Gerard, satisfying your warm desire, and until now I haven't received the slightest answer; it would have therefore assured me of you receiving it.
  I gather this occasion to address a humble prayer in the name of St. Gerard.
  Presently finding the chapel of St. Gerard somewhat damaged of its decorations, caused by the humidity, I have need to restore it, first however, there is need of a large sum of money that the sanctuary in its present condition cannot dispense.
  To that regard, therefore, I warmly pray that you, most Reverend Father gather a few donations among your following to support the great work of St. Gerard, who helps all with the power of miracles.
  I await, therefore, your reply regarding to what I have humbly lowered myself, and anticipating in the name of the Saint, Thaumaturgus wonderworker and the infinite goodness of God from whom we will be compensated. I want St. Gerard to send to you continuously from the heavens, graces and benedictions.
  I send you my respects, and kissing your hand, I entrust your fervid orations of your humble servant of Jesus Christ, Gerardo M. Biscotti, of the most Holy Redeemer, Rector of the Sanctuary

In the early days, the feast was run by the *Societa Fraterno Amore* (Society of Fraternal Love), or the *Fratellanza*, along with other members of the Caposelesi colony. This society predated the existence of the *Societa Maschile San Gerardo Maiella* (St. Gerard Men's Society). On November 10, 1920, the *Societa San Gerardo Maiella Fra i Caposelesi* was incorporated. The incorporation papers state that this corporation was formed to "solicit and collect offers, donations and contributions to Saint Gerardo Maiella and to arrange, perform and carry out a religious celebration each year in the name of San Gerardo Maiella."

According to the incorporation papers of November 10, 1920, the founders of this men's society were Giuseppe Gonnella, Alfonso DelTufo, Baldoino DelGuercio, Luigi Zarra, Gaetano Rosamilia, Pasquale Ruglio, Rocco Rosania, Tommaso Cibelli, Gaetano Fioravanti, Lorenzo Caruso, Pasquale Masi, Alfonso Alefono and Angelo Cibellis.

The officers for the first year in existence were Giuseppe Gonnella, president; Alfonso DelTufo, corresponding secretary; Baldoino DelGuercio, financial secretary; Luigi Zarra, treasurer; Rocco Rosania, trustee; and Gaetano Rosamilia, trustee.

Six years after the St. Gerard Men's Society came into existence, the San Gerardo Maiella Religious Fraternity was formed. "They came into existence on July 29, 1926. Alfonso DelTufo was the President, Giuseppe Chiaravallo, Secretary, Michele Antonelli, Financial Secretary, Camillo Malanga, Treasurer and Alessio Ilaria, Trustee." Eventually, this religious fraternity became extinct.

During the early years, as I have said previously, many customs came into existence. Oftentimes you would see women venerating St. Gerard

Fratellanza, Societa Fraterno Amore, circa 1920s. *Courtesy of the Newark Public Library M. Immerso Collection of the "Old First Ward," Charles F. Cummings New Jersey Information Center, Mr. George Hawley, Supervising Librarian.*

Above, left: Members of the Feast Committee/Society and band in rear, circa 1910. *Courtesy of the Newark Public Library M. Immerso Collection of the "Old First Ward," Charles F. Cummings New Jersey Information Center, Mr. George Hawley, Supervising Librarian.*

Above, right: Statue of St. Gerard with a canopy over it, pictured in 1935. Giuseppe Gonnella pins a donation on the statue, with Rafaella Caprio (left) and Paolo Lanza (right). *Courtesy of the Newark Public Library M. Immerso Collection of the "Old First Ward," Charles F. Cummings New Jersey Information Center, Mr. George Hawley, Supervising Librarian.*

as the patron of mothers and their children (born and unborn). Women would not only carry their children in their arms when requesting his powerful intercession but might also carry a candle. Sometimes it would be a rather large candle carried in thanksgiving for a favor received or prayers answered. The "size or weight of the candles carried in the procession would sometimes be equal to the weight or size of the person, often a child, for whom the Saint was asked to intercede."[15] Another tradition that began early on was the dressing of little children like St. Gerard. There is clear evidence from the early processions of parents showing their gratitude to Almighty God through the powerful intercession of St. Gerard. These children were dressed in a black habit much like the one worn by Redemptorist priests and brothers. This also included the white color, worn around the neck at the top of the black habit, and rosary beads as well.

As one can see, women and children, especially young girls, played a very important role in this outward and demonstrative devotion to St. Gerard during his feast each October. There was in existence before the mid 1920s a women's auxiliary of St. Gerard. They were called the Gerardines after their patronal namesake. On October 17, 1929, the *Newark Evening News* reported that the procession for the Feast of St. Gerard began at 1:00 p.m. and was led by the "Caposelesi Ladies Society, the Gerardines, and the young girl's society moved through the winding streets until 7:00 p.m."

The Gerardines dressed like their namesake in the habit of the Redemptorist Order. In addition to their black habit, white collar and

Above: Young girls dressed as angels carry the hanging baskets with money donations draped over the flowers in the St. Gerard Feast. From the *Sunday Call* October 28, 1923. *Courtesy of the Newark Public Library M. Immerso Collection of the "Old First Ward," Charles F. Cummings New Jersey Information Center, Mr. George Hawley, Supervising Librarian.*

Opposite, top left: Young boy dressed as St. Gerard. Many parents dressed their children in the habit of the Redemptorist Order for the Feast of St. Gerard. *Courtesy of the Newark Public Library M. Immerso Collection of the "Old First Ward," Charles F. Cummings New Jersey Information Center, Mr. George Hawley, Supervising Librarian.*

Opposite, top right: Young boys carrying candles, circa 1920s. *Courtesy of the Newark Public Library M. Immerso Collection of the "Old First Ward," Charles F. Cummings New Jersey Information Center, Mr. George Hawley, Supervising Librarian.*

Opposite, bottom: Priest and devotees carrying candles pose for a photo. *Courtesy of the Newark Public Library M. Immerso Collection of the "Old First Ward," Charles F. Cummings New Jersey Information Center, Mr. George Hawley, Supervising Librarian.*

rosary beads, they wore society badges and ribbons. Because of his special predilection for family life, it was not uncommon to see mothers, fathers and children walking in procession. They carried, as well, the respective banners of the societies they belonged to in honor of St. Gerard.

The *Newark Evening News* reported in the 1920s that "men, children and mothers with baby carriages bent their heads in prayer and followed the procession for hours."

Top left: Young girls dressed as angels carrying the hanging baskets. *Courtesy of the Newark Public Library M. Immerso Collection of the "Old First Ward," Charles F. Cummings New Jersey Information Center, Mr. George Hawley, Supervising Librarian.*

Top right: Young girls carrying the "Gold Box" with jewelry donated by the faithful, with the Gerardines in the background. *Courtesy of the Newark Public Library M. Immerso Collection of the "Old First Ward," Charles F. Cummings New Jersey Information Center, Mr. George Hawley, Supervising Librarian.*

Bottom: Members of the Women's Society were known as the Gerardines. From the *Sunday Call* November 2, 1924. *Courtesy of the Newark Public Library M. Immerso Collection of the "Old First Ward," Charles F. Cummings New Jersey Information Center, Mr. George Hawley, Supervising Librarian.*

Grace Russomanno dressed as an angel for the St. Gerard Feast, circa 1930. *Courtesy of the Newark Public Library M. Immerso Collection of the "Old First Ward," Charles F. Cummings New Jersey Information Center, Mr. George Hawley, Supervising Librarian.*

The "gold box" was another tradition that was alive and well in the 1920s. The "gold box" contained jewelry that was given by the faithful as a gift to St. Gerard when asking for a particular favor or a grace or in thanksgiving for a favor that they received. It could be any piece of gold jewelry—a necklace, gold earrings or a gold watch chain. The jewelry obtained from the faithful was put on the statue of St. Gerard and then later placed in the gold box and carried in procession. Eventually the gold was melted down and used to make one of the halos St. Gerard wears in procession.

Still another beautiful tradition was that of the hanging basket. The hanging basket was ornately decorated with flowers, money and ribbons. The baskets oftentimes were lowered by a cord from a nearby fire escape or a window a few stories above. The basket was lowered in front of St. Gerard as he stopped in the procession route at various devotees' homes. The baskets were then carried in procession by young girls dressed like angels.

Throngs of devotees await the hanging basket being lowered from an apartment above. From the *Sunday Call* November 2, 1924. *Courtesy of the Newark Public Library M. Immerso Collection of the "Old First Ward," Charles F. Cummings New Jersey Information Center, Mr. George Hawley, Supervising Librarian.*

During the procession, devotees also walked barefooted in thanksgiving. They performed acts of penance in return for the special graces they received. "Others came on their knees to the niche where the statue was displayed, and some even licked the ground as they approached the statue."[16] As you have seen, many customs and traditions became common annual practices during the first twenty-five years of our beloved feast of St. Gerard.

Chapter 2

The Glory Years

The first quarter of the twentieth century clearly portrays how the life of St. Lucy's parish and its shepherd, Father Perotti, go hand in hand with the Feast of St. Gerard. Father Perotti committed his life's work to lifting his sheep, which he loved dearly, out of "squalor and poverty." This saintly pastor encountered many obstacles along the way, but that did not stop him, even in the face of difficult problems and adversity. He certainly rose above the situation at hand. He was faced with a very real problem: he had to provide a comfortable, ample-sized spiritual home for his ever-growing flock. His flock was quickly outgrowing the old wooden church that had long served its purpose. He fully realized that something needed to be done; however, he did not have the financial means to build a much-needed larger church, a new St. Lucy's.

The very essence that was an important part of the parishioners' spiritual life was their devotion to the saints. The various groups of Italian immigrants who settled in the "Old First Ward" celebrated the patron saint of their town in Italy in a special way. These feasts were celebrated by the people of the parish with great fervor and devotion. However, there was one drawback that affected the financial well-being of the parish. The problem was that these feasts were organized and controlled by the various societies from where the people came from in Italy. For example, there was the St. Gerard Men's Society, the Fratellanza, the San Nicola Society, the St. Anthony Society, the San Donato Society, the San Sabino Society, the Society of Our Lady of Mt. Carmel and the San Michele Society. Each one of these societies organized and controlled the feast of their patron saint from their town in Italy.

Interestingly, although these parishioners of St. Lucy's were quite poor, to say the least, they supported each one of these feasts in a very generous manner. The one very important drawback was that, the church, which met all of their spiritual needs, did not reap the financial benefit that it so desperately needed to construct a new house of worship. In fact, the church received very little financial support from each of these feasts. The pastor even tried to suspend the feasts so that he could raise enough money to build a new church because of the pressure he received from individual societies.

In addition to all that went on in parish life (daily masses, weekend masses, novenas, parish missions, confession, baptisms, weddings, meetings of parish societies and organizations and curates assisting the pastor in shepherding the flock), the pastor and his assistants opened the doors of the church and led the faithful in their treasured celebrations of their feasts honoring the saint of their paese.

St. Gerard Feast with throngs of devotees present. The St. Gerard statue appears inside the circle. *Courtesy of the archives of the Museum of the "Old First Ward" of Newark, Curator, Mr. Bob Cascella.*

50

The Glory Years

Newspapers of the day reporting on the feast of St. Gerard stated that prior to the feast, there was a nine-day novena in honor of St. Gerard. During the feast itself, there were solemn high masses and other masses throughout the morning. Italian-speaking priests from the diocese, outside the diocese and outside the country came to give the *panegerico* (a long, detailed sermon on the life and virtues of the saint). Sometimes a priest would come from Italy. Usually, it would be a priest from the town where the society was from.

At 1:00 p.m. each day during the feast, the priests and altar boys, along with the various societies, prepared for the outdoor procession through the neighborhood. The highlight of the day came when the statue of the saint was carried out of the church while the faithful devotees anxiously awaited his presence so the procession could commence. In the evening, after the procession, the church provided the faithful with solemn vespers and benediction of the most blessed sacrament.

In October 1929, the *Newark Evening News* reported that

> *about 6,000 Italian-Americans thronged Sheffield Street last night to hear a band concert, the concluding feature of an elaborate celebration in honor of St. Gerard, which opened with a solemn high mass in St. Lucy's Roman Catholic Church yesterday morning and continued with a colorful procession that lasted seven hours.*
>
> *The band stood beneath a model façade of an ancient Venetian Cathedral, erected for the occasion in font of St. Lucy's Church. Seventy-two musicians played, directed by two leaders. The program consisted of airs from Italian operas and sacred music. The façade was illuminated by arches of almond, green, white lights.*
>
> *Arthur Tuccino of New York in a speech declared the Italians were fortunate to have two holidays such as Columbus and St. Gerard days so close together. The band played until midnight...*

During this time period, one of Father Perotti's assistants, Father Gaetano Ruggiero, was to play a key role not only in the Feast of St. Gerard but also in the very life of St. Lucy's parish and its future course and direction. Ruggiero had been Perotti's assistant from 1922 to 1931. During this time, Perotti relied heavily on his curate to assist him with the spiritual needs of the parish. These two priests, who were different in many ways, became good friends as well.

Keep in mind that Father Perotti was born in northern Italy, while Father Ruggiero was born in Sicily and possessed a more worldly character.

Left to right: Reverend Serafino Donzillo, Monsignor J. Perotti and Reverend Gaetano Ruggiero. From St. Lucy's archives. *Courtesy of the Newark Public Library M. Immerso Collection of the "Old First Ward," Charles F. Cummings New Jersey Information Center, Mr. George Hawley, Supervising Librarian.*

Ruggiero was a chaplain in the army in Italy and held a doctorate in canon law. On the other hand, Perotti was a simple, holy parish priest, "even tempered and gentle," while Ruggiero was "exceptionally strong willed and a skilled administrator."[17]

Prior to and during Ruggiero's tenure as Perotti's associate, the saintly pastor knew that his flock needed a larger church to accommodate the ever-growing needs of the parish. Interestingly, the parish census of 1920 revealed that there were 17,000 parishioners, and their number was growing. There were more than 10,000 baptisms prior to the census of that year. Notably, there were 1,110 baptisms recorded in one year.

The parish had certainly grown and come a long way since 1900 when land was secured for the church and school. With this growing population ever present to him, the future and present needs of the parish weighed heavily on the pastor's mind. Although he had no money to speak of, Father Perotti began to formalize his plans. A decision was made on May 29, 1918, to launch a campaign for a fund drive. However, the campaign did not get off the ground until May 21, 1923. In 1923, the pastor built a parish hall to serve as a temporary house of worship until the new and much needed church was ready. The ground was formally broken on May 3, 1925, with an official ceremony.

At this time, the old wooden church that had long outlived its usefulness was demolished to make way for the new magnificent church we have today. The new church was ready by 1926, although the interior remained incomplete. As of 1926, there were no stained-glass windows or any windows at all for the new church.

On December 13, 1926, the Feast of St. Lucy, the church was consecrated. Bishop Thomas Walsh officiated at the dedication ceremony of the new church on July 22, 1928.

The groundbreaking ceremony for St. Lucy's Church took place on May 3, 1925. *Courtesy of the Newark Public Library M. Immerso Collection of the "Old First Ward," Charles F. Cummings New Jersey Information Center, Mr. George Hawley, Supervising Librarian.*

The old wooden church, circa early twentieth century. *Courtesy of the archives of the Museum of the "Old First Ward" of Newark, Curator, Mr. Bob Cascella.*

The Glory Years

Above: Interior of the new church during the Christmas season. *Courtesy of the archives of Reverend Thomas D. Nicastro Jr.*

Opposite, top: Groundbreaking of the new church, circa 1920s. *Courtesy of the archives of the Museum of the "Old First Ward" of Newark, Curator, Mr. Bob Cascella.*

Opposite, bottom: Exterior of the new church—circa late 1920s. *Courtesy of the archives of the Museum of the "Old First Ward" of Newark, Curator, Mr. Bob Cascella.*

Due to the Depression and lack of funds, Perotti had to focus his attention fully on the needs of his struggling parishioners. For several years, the interior of the new church remained incomplete. The year 1929 saw the founding of the St. Vincent DePaul Society for those in financial distress. At this point, he felt compelled to devote himself totally to his poor flock as they struggled through some very tough times. In due time, all good things come to those who wait, but for now, the church building would be without windows, and the interior would remain incomplete. Eventually, this magnificent church would be completed with beautiful stained-glass windows, marble from Italy and breathtaking murals painted by Italian artisans from the old country. For the moment, the emphasis was not on the church building, the physical structure, but rather on the members of the mystical body of Christ, a worshiping community of Roman Catholics giving worship to God, the Holy Trinity and veneration to God's heavenly heroes, the saints.

Interior of the new church prior to its completion with marble, stained-glass windows and murals on the ceiling, circa 1930, photo from St. Lucy's archives. *Courtesy of the archives of the Museum of the "Old First Ward" of Newark, Curator, Mr. Bob Cascella.*

Time was marching on, and our dear Father Perotti's earthly ministry as a priest was coming to a close. In 1931, at the request of Bishop Thomas Walsh, the Holy Father elevated Father Joseph Perotti to the rank of monsignor in recognition for all his work on behalf of the Italian immigrants in Newark's Little Italy. He gave everything he had away and was always generous to the poor and to parishioners in need. So great was his generosity that he never thought about himself or saving for his future. When he was elevated to the rank of monsignor; he couldn't even afford to purchase the ecclesiastical attire for the rank of monsignor; it had to be purchased for him by his grateful benefactors. Despite all the turmoil of the late 1920s and early 1930s, the Feast of St. Gerard continued as it always had. Now as the pastor was getting older, he relied more and more on his associate, Father Gaetano Ruggiero. He assisted Father Perotti in participating in the procession for the feast each year.

After his elevation to the rank of monsignor, Perotti lived another two years. In the last year of his earthly life, he completed another construction project for the Italian Catholic Union (the ICU). However, he did not live to see the church he built and hoped for fully completed. That responsibility would fall in divine providence to Monsignor Perotti's successor, associate

Interior of the new church during the Christmas season. Monsignor Perotti stands near the *presepio* (nativity scene), circa late 1920s. *Courtesy of the archives of the Museum of the "Old First Ward" of Newark, Curator, Mr. Bob Cascella.*

and friend, Father Gaetano Ruggiero. The very same year he completed his last major project, the ICU Building, the beloved shepherd and people's priest, the saintly Monsignor Perotti, died. He collapsed while saying mass and went home to his eternal reward on September 14, 1933.

Truly this young parish suffered a great loss with the death of its first permanent shepherd and pastor. One can safely say that the entire First Ward mourned this great loss. It was reported that approximately three thousand people attended Monsignor Perotti's funeral. The church was filled to capacity, and the streets outside were filled with his beloved parishioners

Above: The funeral of Monsignor Joseph Perotti, first pastor of St. Lucy's. *Courtesy of the Newark Public Library M. Immerso Collection of the "Old First Ward," Charles F. Cummings New Jersey Information Center, Mr. George Hawley, Supervising Librarian.*

Opposite, top: Funeral of Monsignor Perotti at Holy Sepulchre Cemetery, September 14, 1933. *Courtesy of Rodolfo Colamedici family archives.*

Opposite, bottom: Presepio (nativity scene) at St. Lucy's, with Monsignor Perotti in front, circa late 1920s or early 1930s. *Courtesy of Rodolfo Colamedici family archives.*

hoping to pay their respects and get a last glimpse of the simple parish priest they revered as a "living saint."

Bishop Walsh was so convinced of this priest's holiness that he said in his sermon in which he eulogized Perotti, "We are burying a Saint today." He further stated that anyone was welcome to see proof, if they needed it, by visiting the stark room that he called home. He was noted for giving all his earthly possessions away. Others came first before himself. It was said that when he died, all he possessed were the clothes on his back and fifty cents. Monsignor Perotti was laid to rest, after the funeral mass that attracted

throngs of people, at Holy Sepulchre Cemetery. Even his burial plot had to be donated by two grateful parishioners.

By the time of his death, St. Lucy's had grown in leaps and bounds from "two thousand to thirty five thousand members."[18] That was certainly quite an accomplishment. Perotti's earthly task of shepherding was now complete. St. Lucy's would now begin a new chapter in its service to God's holy people. The year 1933 was significant in the life of the St. Gerard Feast. It was the formation and organization of the Circolo Progressivo Caposelesi or C.P.C. Club. This organization was incorporated three years later on September 20, 1936. The original intention of the early founders of this organization was the desire to create a guild of tailors from Caposele. They had a special love for St. Gerard since he himself was a tailor and lived the last year of his earthly life at the monastery of Caposele (Materdomini).

The original founders were Alfonso DiMaio, Eliseo Caprio, Antonio Chiaravallo, Gabriele Caprio, Beniamino Scolavino, Salvatore Merola and Gerardo LaManna. Originally, to be a member of this club, one had to be not only from Caposele but also a tailor as well. However, fifteen years after its beginning, all those of Caposelesi origin were admitted as members, and then in 1964 "membership was opened up to all who cherish progress and tradition."[19] Basically, this organization became one of the groups that not only solicited funds for the feast but also ran the feast of St. Gerard until it was taken over by the church, under the pastorate of Father Gaetano Ruggiero.

Because of the ever-growing popular devotion to St. Gerard, it was decided that an annex would be added to the beautiful church of St. Lucy, and so in 1933, the same year of Monsignor Perotti's death, construction began on the St. Gerard chapel that would be called the Sanctuary of St. Gerard.

In 1934, Father Ruggiero took the reins as the second pastor of St. Lucy's. Father Ruggiero was left with a huge debt from his predecessor's projects but was determined to put the parish back "in good financial order." Without a doubt, Ruggiero was very different from Perotti, as shown by his "strong will and determined nature."

Keep in mind that Ruggiero was Perotti's assistant for a good number of years and observed the interactions between the church and the various societies that ran all the many feasts held at St. Lucy's. He saw firsthand how the people contributed generously to the feast of their patron saint. These societies controlled every aspect of the feast; the church was in no way in control. Ruggiero knew this, but he couldn't do anything about it. When he became pastor, all that was about to change. He once said, in reference to Perotti, "In all charity…he was a very saintly, holy priest, but he was no administrator."

The Glory Years

In retrospect, Father Ruggiero really saved the day. He had the courage and the foresight to realize that if he wanted to put the church in good financial standing and secure the survival of these feasts—in particular, the great feast of St. Gerard—then the church had to take complete control of everything. He realized that with each passing year, the Feast of St. Gerard; in particular, was not only very well attended and growing but also that its income was multiplying. Further, he realized that this income was necessary to complete the church edifice, as well as other important projects.

Again with great courage, wisdom and foresight, he decided to put an end to society-controlled feasts. He believed that the church should be the one to direct and guide the people in these religious and devotional practices. It certainly was an uphill battle for him; it wasn't easy, to say the least. The members of these societies weren't going to take this parochial act lightly. He was reported to the bishop and diocesan officials via letters of protest. But he stood firm and didn't waver, even in the face of grave opposition. Why? Because he knew that this action would ensure the survival of the feast and would be of great importance to the parish. "Despite vehement objections, including a threat against his life, Ruggiero prevailed."[20]

It is worth noting that "his (Ruggiero's) insistence that the feasts be held under the auspices of the Church, assured the survival of the parish, by securing a source of income when a number of active parishioners began to decline."[21]

Yes, we owe a huge debt of gratitude to this man's courage, wisdom and vision of the future in assuring the survival not only of the feast of great St. Gerard, but also the means to keep this beautiful church functioning even through the decline of the old neighborhood. The church directed everything; the societies were welcomed and could participate annually, but the church would be the sole beneficiary of all these feasts. Due to Ruggiero's guidance, leadership and administrative skills, the Feast of St. Gerard flourished throughout the 1930s, '40s and '50s.

One could easily characterize the period between the 1890s and the early part of the 1950s as the glory years of the "Old First Ward." Newark's Little Italy was certainly a magical, wonderful place to live. One could safely say that the old neighborhood was the most colorful and interesting during the feast season.

Coming from a European mindset and tradition, the family unit was an important component of the immigrant's life as well as their devotion to the saints. These immigrants, especially southern Italians living in Newark's

The Feast of Saint Gerard Maiella, C.Ss.R.

Little Italy, expressed their Catholic faith and, in particular, their devotion to the saints, in a very demonstrative manner. This expression of devotion was foreign and, at times, uncomfortable to immigrants of other ethnic backgrounds. What they intended to do was recreate as faithfully as possible the feast day and celebration of the patron saint of their town in Italy.

> *To the more sophisticated, the images, and superstitions, the festivals, processions and feasts that formed the daily religious life of an immigrant seemed to reflect a pagan, rather than Christian, tradition. Many devout Italians, however, perceived these customs to be essential to worship and to the maintenance of tradition. In fact, what critics saw as a departure from the church was, in part, an adjustment of old world traditions to new surroundings in America.[22]*

For those who are familiar with the feast season in the "Old First Ward," one could easily say that it was a special time like no other. Each different *paese* had its own statue of its heavenly patron which community members sent for from the Old Country.

This was a time when all the members of a particular town came together as one big family to make the necessary preparations for the big day. Each society, prior to the church taking over, was responsible for all the expenses. The members had to hire the band and the vendors for the street festival, make the decorations, put up the streetlights, arrange for the fireworks display and secure the priest, sometimes a priest from their town in Italy, to give the *panegerico* and arrange for the solemn high mass. The church was decorated inside and out. On the outside, they would erect a facade of their church in Italy.

"The narrow streets surrounding St. Lucy's Church were adorned with arches of multi-colored electric lights (lampadine) and small baskets of flowers. At one time the colorful street arches were lighted with glass globes containing oil wicks."[23]

The decorations included ten thousand oil lamps. Newspapers of the day were reporting that there was clear evidence that the Feast of St. Gerard and the outdoor festival celebration were quite large and extensive. *Bancarelle* (concession stands) were set up by Sheffield Street and Eighth Avenue and similar ones on Eighth facing Seventh Avenue, while a number of the other streets were decorated on a large scale that included bunting and flags. Bandstands were erected to accommodate the bands for the feast. Naturally, the band concerts in the evening and the elaborate fireworks display were an integral part of the evening celebrations. It was said that thousands enjoyed the concert at night. The nighttime orchestras included over one hundred pieces. As the faithful devotees walked in procession, one could easily view the elaborate arch over the roadway at Eighth and Summer Avenues. House decorations were elaborate, numerous and picturesque, to say the least.

The *Newark Evening Star* reported that the feast of St. Gerard was "one of the most important on the Italian Calendar and those preparations…were larger than ever before." Interestingly, it said that during the procession, "business among the Italians was discarded."

Many a person will recall those yesteryears when we experienced the sights and sounds, the music coming from Campione's band and the smells and aromas emanating from the bancarelle. Do you remember the concerts by night, when the orchestra played and Italian tenors sang pieces form various operas and delighted throngs of people with those old, familiar Neapolitan classics? What about the special effects of the fireworks display when the technicians were able to reproduce a likeness of the saint's image in the night sky?

The highlight and joy of every feast was the procession with the statue of the saint. The procession usually commenced around 1:00 p.m., after the Solemn High Mass. The saint was carried out of the church by the society members to the sound of the band and the fireworks going off announcing the arrival of the sacred image coming to greet the faithful devotees. The procession was led by the band, followed by the societies with their banners, then the priests and altar boys followed by the Guard of Honor closest to the saint.

The processions themselves were colorful, with the faithful carrying flags and candles of various sizes. There were, of course, those who made vows to St. Gerard who walked either barefooted or in stocking feet in thanksgiving for favors received. Along the way, the procession would stop at each of the homes of the faithful as they pinned their offering on the statue or gave their jewelry. The arrival of the saint at your family home was the most important thing. If it was Sunday and you were cooking, boiling water for the macaroni (a staple food of Italians on all Sundays, including Sundays during the feast), you stopped. Everything stopped, as the entire family, young and old, gathered outside the old family home, decorated for the arrival of a dignitary, to greet the venerable statue of St. Gerard as it passed by. Family members would refer to him as a real person and not speak in terms of a statue. This is interesting to note. One cannot deny that each of these stops were very moving as members of the family prayed or conversed with the saint or as *nonna* (grandma) sang hymns of devotion from the old country to him. Some members of the family would release real doves in front of the Saint or shower him with rose petals.

The feast season at St. Lucy's was lengthy. Beginning in the month of June with the Feast of St. Anthony, feasts were held every other week throughout the summer until the fall with the colorful feast of St. Michael the Archangel in September. Then the feast season ended in October with the greatest feast of all, the Feast of St. Gerard, which went out in a ray of spectacular and grand celebration.

In October 1929, the *Newark News* reported that the St. Gerard Feast was the last of ten feasts celebrated at St. Lucy's. Some of the feasts celebrated at St. Lucy's at one time or another in the "Old First Ward" were St. Anthony, Our Lady of Sorrows, St. Rocco, San Nicola, San Donato, San Sebastiano, San Sabino, La Madonna della Assunta, San Michele and San Gerardo. One of the most colorful feasts was San Michele (St. Michael) with the Flight of the Angels (*Volo degli Angeli*).

St. Michael's Feast committee. *Courtesy of the archives of the Museum of the "Old First Ward" of Newark, Curator, Mr. Bob Cascella.*

The Glory Years

At the beginning and end of the procession of St. Michael, young girls dressed as angels in white were hoisted onto a rope with a pulley. The harness was hidden under their makeshift wings attached to the pulley that moved them along a rope high above the street from one end to the other. As they moved along, they asked the crowd of devotees for silence as they recited prayers to their heavenly patron and then shouted, "Viva San Michele!" (Long live St. Michael!) After the recitation of prayers, they released doves and flower petals in front of the statue of the saint.

Even with all the color and pageantry of all these feasts, the feast of St. Gerard always closed the feast season with much pageantry. With each new year, the Feast of St. Gerard was growing larger and larger—so much so that the devotion to him was nothing less than phenomenal.

A baptismal certificate belonging to Filomena Maria Miano from the 1930s gives us clear proof of the importance of St. Gerard in the parish life at St. Lucy's. The official name on the certificate reads *"Chiesa di Santa Lucia, Santuario di San Gerardo"* (Church of St. Lucy, Sanctuary of St. Gerard). Other baptismal certificates from that era give proof of this as well.

The parish record of August 9, 1926 states the full name of the parish and that permission was granted "first that the official title and patroness of the church is St. Lucy, Second—the name of St. Gerard be added as follows: Sanctuary of St. Gerard or Shrine of St. Gerard."[24]

In 1935, St. Gerard's Sanctuary was solemnly dedicated on October 16. A solemn pontifical mass was celebrated by Bishop Thomas J. Walsh. The altar of St. Gerard was consecrated on Tuesday, October 15 by Monsignor Thomas R. McLaughlin. Those in attendance at the mass were the pastor, Reverend Gaetano Ruggiero, and Reverend Ferdinand Anzelone, pastor of St. Nicholas Palisades, the Archpriest of the mass.

The deacons were Reverend Joseph Ferrecchia of St. Nicholas Church and Reverend Achille Rondinara, curate of St. Lucy's. The subdeacon was Reverend Salvatore Medaglia, pastor of Our Lady of Mount Carmel, Montclair, and the master of ceremonies was Monsignor John G. Delaney, administrator of St. Patrick's Cathedral. The Reverend Walter Artioli, pastor of Our Lady of Mount Carmel, Jersey City, was the assistant master of ceremonies. Reverend Umberto Bonuomo of New York preached the *panegerico*.

The chapel of St. Gerard, located on the southern side of the church, is Romanesque in style, with a sixteenth-century chandelier hanging in the center. The chandelier, which comes from a Roman home, was donated by Vita Mariani of Newark.

Interior of the new church, with original High Altar, prior to the completion of the church. *Courtesy of the archives of the Museum of the "Old First Ward" of Newark, Curator, Mr. Bob Cascella.*

The Sanctuary of St. Gerard was designed by Luigi Vivoli of Grantwood, New Jersey.

From 1941 to 1945; America was involved in the Second World War. Hundreds of young men who lived in the First Ward went off to war to fight for their country. Some were lucky enough to be assigned overseas in Italy and were given a golden opportunity to visit the hometowns of their parents. It was a great chance to meet their Italian relatives and see where it all began. During the war, the feast continued but "lights were curtailed at night," as explained in the 1999 documentary about the feast. The faithful devotees still walked in procession and invoked their heavenly patron to safely return home their sons, brothers and all relatives from war.

After the dedication of the St. Gerard Sanctuary, the feast continued to grow with each passing year. Father Ruggiero set his focus on completing the interior of the new church as we know it today. It was completed with marble and beautiful stained-glass windows from Europe. The murals on the ceiling were completed in 1948, under the direction of Professor Gonippo Raggi. Raggi also worked on the interior of the Cathedral Basilica of the Sacred Heart. After the completion of the church, the pastor turned his

The Glory Years

focus on St. Gerard's Chapel, which was already dedicated but not fully decorated until Easter 1949.

Around Easter 1948, Father Ruggiero sent out a letter in Italian and English concerning raising money to decorate St. Gerard's Shrine. Interestingly, he notes in the letter that "St. Gerard's Shrine was not included in the decoration [when St. Lucy's Church was decorated]. That was purposely done. It was indeed my intention to make of it something really special and worthy of that architectural jewel that it is and of the deep devotion of many devotees of our dear St. Gerard."

He stated that "the exquisite work will amount to a considerable sum" and that it would be ready by the next Easter, 1949.

Although not dated, we can determine from the tone of the letter that it was written and sent out in 1948 around Easter. He asked the faithful devotees for a generous offering according to their means and interestingly makes clear that only the parish priests and himself were authorized to solicit and collect funds for this project. He said, "Any donations should be sent or handed to me or to one of the parish priests." He then signed the letter as pastor.

During these years, crowds would gather and walk the procession. The traditions continued with the priests and altar boys walking with the saint in procession throughout the day and evening. It is amazing how time marches on. Our beautiful feast of St. Gerard has already reached its first fifty years with the close of the feast of 1949.

Paraphrasing Geta Spatola, president of the St. Gerard Ladies Guild, from her interview for the St. Gerard documentary on the 100th anniversary, she states that the first half of the history of the feast up until the 1950s was a celebration ethnic in nature as well as religious, but then in the second half of the feast's history, things changed, the feast and neighborhood alike. It was

Exterior of the new church. *Courtesy of the archives of the Museum of the "Old First Ward" of Newark, Curator, Mr. Bob Cascella.*

no longer just a religious expression of the Patron Saint of Caposele but also a celebration of St. Gerard as patron of mothers, the unborn and babies.

Undoubtedly, the first fifty years of the feast can be characterized by saying they were ethnic in nature, however, the second fifty years would become more diverse in character, scope, devotion and significance. New customs and traditions blended with older ones. The one constant, however, is the devotion to the St. Gerard. As we move into the second fifty years of the centennial celebration, we see that some time-honored traditions carry over and continue.

Women continue to play a dominant role in the devotion, procession and celebration of the feast. Members of the Women's Auxiliary of St. Gerard still carry banners with the assistance of young children who were also devotees of St. Gerard. The societies continue to walk in procession, expressing outwardly their love and devotion.

The tradition of people walking barefoot or in stocking feet, especially women, continued to manifest itself during the procession in the 1950s. The members of the band played those old familiar hymns that express our devotion. They continue to be an integral part of the festivities and celebration.

In gratitude for favors received from St. Gerard, parents still continued to dress their children in the black habit of the Redemptorist Order.

The tradition of pinning the money on the saint continued as well. With each passing year, the capes of money got larger and larger. At some of the stops along the procession route, devotees still continued to release doves to fly around St. Gerard as the faithful showered him with flower petals.

Part and parcel to the feast was the celebration aspect; the concession stands (bancarelle) along with decorations and streetlights still continued. Now that the war was over, the streets were lit up brightly each evening with multicolor illumination. People continued to enjoy the nuts and torrone candy, the clams, sausage and peppers, zeppole, calzones and other delicious treats.

During the 1950s, throngs of people continued to walk for hours in procession singing, praying the rosary and enjoying the company of relatives and friends. Children, as well as men and women, continued to manifest their great love for St. Gerard by erecting homemade shrines in front of their homes with replicas of St. Gerard's statue (in particular, our beloved statue at St. Lucy's). Houses were ornately decorated with pictures of St. Gerard (*i quadri*) beautifully framed and displayed with flowers, candles, streamers and bunting. Added to this were the sounds of hymns to the saint coming from record players inside the homes.

The Glory Years

Those who were and still are an important component of the Feast of St. Gerard are the men who belonged to the Guard of Honor. The members of this organization were appointed by the pastor to assist him in the church as ushers and greeters. Their main function was to assist in taking up the collection at Sunday masses and on Holy Days of Obligation. They assisted with various functions around the church, in the community center and in the chapel of St. Gerard. During the Feast of St. Gerard, they assisted at all the masses, took up the collection and did their best to coordinate the throngs of people making their way to St. Gerard's Chapel. Before the procession began, they pinned the money on the statue and carried the saint out of the church for the procession. During the procession, four members at a time rode the cart with the statue to assist the faithful in pinning their annual donation. Their presence, dedication and faithfulness were truly an asset to St. Lucy's parish life.

The following are the deceased members of the Guard of Honor:

Cosmo Alagna, Armando Alagna, Anthony Armellino, Fred Biunno, Thomas Campione, Michael Corbo, Philip Gesualdo, Anthony Manocchio, Vincent Mattia, Fred Matullo, Philip Mercurio, Nicholas Mescia, Henry Naddeo, Ralph Nicastro, Thomas Pescatore, Joseph Picone, Michael Pompilio, Fiore Porcaro, Frank Rosania, Salvatore Rosania, Marty Rossi, Rocco Rotunda, Ralph Sangiovanni, John Sierchio, Dr. Michael Soriano, Joseph Soriano, Louis Tipaldi, John Tortorello, Ralph Tribelli, Anthony Tubello, Frank Conrad, Confessor Gomez, Dennis Mercurio, William Morgan, Rocco Tomaselli, Arsenio Saporito, John Faiella, Emil Gianfrancisco, Frank Bonassi, Anthony Coppola and Stephen Mercurio.

The following are the present active members of the Guard of Honor:

Robert Adams, Simplice Ahoua, Nicholas Battista, Joseph Battista, Zachery Bozza, Vito Capece, Robert Cascella, Joseph Cerrigione, Stephen Colucci, Nick D'Uva, Joseph DeBlasio, John DiMilia, Sal Fede, Michael Foggio, Raymond Gallicchio, Dennis Genuario, Walter Genuario, Angelo Guida, John Guida, Fred Hornlein, David Laracuente, Jaime Lozada, Luis Maldonado, Gerald Napoliello, Vito Nappi, Vito Nole, Robert Orcinola, Anthony Pascucci, Thomas Pescatore, Peter Petrozzino, Nick Rizzitello, Darin Smith, Anthony Svehla, Anthony Tortorello, Dennis Tucci, Vincent Vespucci, Joseph Viscido and Frank Zarro.

In the following chapter, we will explore the decline of the "Old First Ward" and how St. Lucy's Church and the Feast of St. Gerard held the life of the ward and the Italian colony together as its strong anchor.

Chapter 3

The Decline of the Ward and Its Anchor

St. Lucy's Church and the Venerable Feast of Saint Gerard

After the Second World War, the "Old First Ward" was bustling with activity once again. The feasts at St. Lucy's were as great as ever. Although things seemed to be going well, the old neighborhood was changing. The immigrants who were once a thriving part of the Old Italian neighborhood (colony) were now getting older, and some had gone to their eternal reward. Interestingly, these immigrants and their families were becoming more and more Americanized. The young men who had gone off to war were now returning home, getting married and moving out of the ward to the suburbs.

During the holidays, they would return home to family and friends to celebrate Thanksgiving, Christmas, New Year's Day and Easter. Naturally, they would purchase goods and Italian specialties from the stores along Seventh and Eighth Avenues. Most importantly, many remained loyal to St. Lucy's Church, the hub of the Italian people's spiritual and social life, as well as loyal to the devotion to St. Gerard and the other saints from various paesi.

Although everything seemed to be calm and peaceful in the old neighborhood, things were about to change. There was a big surprise in January 1952, a surprise that shocked and eventually devastated many families in the ward. A large section of the once thriving neighborhood was slated for a federal government project known as urban renewal. This earth-shattering event dealt a great blow to the Italian populace and forever changed their neighborhood, the "Old First Ward." This devastating event probably could have taken place sooner because developers in the federal government already had in mind this type of project in the 1930s. However,

The Decline of the Ward and Its Anchor

Arial view of "Old First Ward." *Courtesy of the Newark Public Library M. Immerso Collection of the "Old First Ward," Charles F. Cummings New Jersey Information Center, Mr. George Hawley, Supervising Librarian.*

plans were put on hold until after the war, when the government started choosing sites around the country.

> *The redevelopment area stretched from Clifton to Broad Street and from Seventh Avenue to State Street. It covered 46 acres and had the highest housing density of any district in the city. Almost every building in the redevelopment zone (about 470 structures) would eventually be razed, replaced with eight twelve story, low income apartment building—the Columbus Homes—at the center of the tract and three privately funded middle incomes high-rise apartment building at the Clifton Avenue and Broad Street ends.*[25]

And so, as one can see, this urban renewal project of the federal government would take away a good portion of this once thriving "Little Italy" of Newark. Unfortunately, very few things were left untouched. St. Lucy's Church and the buildings connected with it remained intact, along with McKinley School and Giordano's Bakery.

Residents tried to stop this disaster, but the plan was supported by many of the leading figures in the Italian community. However, they didn't fully understand the concept and the problems it would eventually cause for so many. Some were misled and didn't fully grasp the scale of the project until it was too late.

The pastor of St. Lucy's at the time, Father Gaetano Ruggiero, thought the project would give his parishioners better housing so they could stay in the old neighborhood. However, when he saw what it would really do, it deeply affected him for many years.

Many were just thrown out against their will. These were dark days for the once thriving, now vanished, "Old First Ward."

Tragedy officially struck in July 1953, and the neighborhood underwent several phases over the next few years. It was a nightmare like no other. One by one, each of those famous streets began to disappear. Businesses that were family owned and operated for generations were forced to leave everything behind. Many were very angry and upset, to say the least.

Statue in procession with Father Ruggiero and young boy in front of statue, (Joe Liloia). From the *Sunday Call* October 23, 1927. *Courtesy of the Newark Public Library M. Immerso Collection of the "Old First Ward," Charles F. Cummings New Jersey Information Center, Mr. George Hawley, Supervising Librarian.*

Some 1,300 families were displaced. People who had lived there since they came from the Old Country and who made a new home in this so-called slum of a neighborhood were now told they had to get out and go elsewhere to start all over again. Those who were affected the most were the elderly, our grandparents and great-grandparents, who lived nearby the church, the very heart of the neighborhood, their beloved St. Lucy's.

After the Columbus Homes opened in August 1955, some came back to live, but most were gone forever with the vanishing neighborhood. Father Ruggiero decided to take a census in hopes to include those living in the Columbus homes. "But in the end, the scale of the buildings overwhelmed what was left of the old neighborhood. Rather than stabilize the community,

Above: Demolition of the "Old First Ward" with St. Lucy's Church in the background. *Courtesy of the Newark Public Library M. Immerso Collection of the "Old First Ward," Charles F. Cummings New Jersey Information Center, Mr. George Hawley, Supervising Librarian.*

Left: Exterior of the new church after demolition of the "Old First Ward," circa 1955. *Courtesy of the archives of the Museum of the "Old First Ward" of Newark, Curator, Mr. Bob Cascella.*

urban renewal hastened its deterioration."[26] Further, "the coming of the Columbus Homes marked the beginning of a long torturous decline from which the First Ward never rebounded."[27]

The decline could have threatened the devotion of parishioners, but it did not. The legacy was maintained despite the difficulties that prevailed. The decline in the neighborhood marked a change socially and politically but not in the spiritual commitment of the devotees. Catholicism and their devotion to the Church permeated the cultural life of Italians. This presence of devotion is striking in the outward display of walking and singing in the procession to celebrate the feast of St. Gerard.

Amidst the neighborhood vanishing, we have one of the few happy occasions that brings all First Warders together, the great Feast of St. Gerard. No one would argue that the one constant that remains unchanged and timeless in the vanishing Little Italy of Newark is the Church of St. Lucy, the hub of devotion to St. Gerard Maiella in the United States.

Unfortunately, all of the other feasts at St. Lucy's did not have the following and the vast and ever-growing numbers of devotees that St. Gerard had. Actually, with each passing year, the devotion to St. Gerard continued to grow in leaps and bounds. Every year, people came from all over the United States to celebrate St. Gerard's Feast and invoke his powerful intercession before God.

Although there were many other feasts at St. Lucy's, their devoted faithful either grew old and died or simply moved away, and their feasts and celebrations died also. Somehow, because of St. Gerard's special predilection for mothers and their children, the feast of this great wonderworker of the eighteenth century endured with the test of time.

Throughout the 1950s, in the midst of all the changes in the world and the old neighborhood, women still carried their society banners and still dressed in the habit of St. Gerard and walked in the processions.

The processions in the mid 1950s reflected the changing neighborhood with the now towering Columbus Homes in the background. Amidst the changing face of the old "Little Italy" of the First Ward, there arrived two young assistants on the scene at St. Lucy's Church, adding a breath of fresh air to the parish life. These two newly ordained priests came to St. Lucy's within a year of one another between 1955 and 1956.

Realizing that the years were passing by and that he would need new, young blood to assist him in his arduous tasks, Father Ruggiero prayed that he would find the right priests to assist him in his work with the Italian apostolate at St. Lucy's. He got his wish. In 1955, Father Joseph Granato arrived on the scene at St. Lucy's, filled with zeal and ready to begin his work with the Italian community at the parish. In his first year at St. Lucy's, Father Granato worked with the Drum and Bugle Corp., the C.Y.O. and the Sodality. Little did he realize that he would someday succeed Father Ruggiero as the third pastor of St. Lucy's Church.

Less than a year after Father Granato's arrival, another young priest, newly ordained and of Italian descent, arrived as another gift to Father Ruggiero. He was Father Joseph Nativo, or as he was affectionately called, Father Nat. Upon his arrival, he assumed the responsibilities of the Drum & Bugle Corp., the C.Y.O. and the Sodality, taking over from Father Granato.

Father Nativo recalls, "I felt young myself and felt I could work with young people, perhaps more successfully than I could do other things. If I could help some young people that would be worthwhile."[28]

Shortly after his arrival, Father Nativo began the St. Lucy's Men's Choir in 1956. This choir would go on to become renowned throughout the Archdiocese of Newark for its unique sound.

A young Father Granato blessing the statue of St. Gerard at the Caposelesi Club on Bloomfield Avenue, Newark. Also shown in photo is Jerry Spatola, president of the club. *Courtesy of the Spatola family archives.*

When asked why he began an all-male choir, Father Nativo responded, "The persuasive reason for starting the choir was the talent of the young men of the parish. In the old rectory, before air conditioning, the sounds of singing coming from the street would drift in through the open windows. Why not bring that sound and that talent into the Church?"[29]

The choir for approximately the first decade of its existence was under the direction of Father Nativo. He was followed by Jerry DeGrazio, who led and directed the choir for over twenty-five years. Jerry DiNola was directing the choir when it entered the twenty-first century. "The choir is a very special part of the parish liturgical celebrations."[30]

During the church's liturgical year, the choir plays an integral part of all the holiday celebrations, especially at Christmas, Holy Week and Easter. In addition to this, they sing for Confirmation and other special occasions. Each Sunday, they faithfully lend their harmonious voices to sing the 11:00 a.m. Mass. Traditionally they would sing during the annual celebration of the Feast of St. Gerard at all the Solemn High Masses. How could anyone forget how beautifully the choir sang the traditional hymn to St. Gerard with love and devotion?

After his arrival in the 1950s, Father Joseph Nativo was asked by Father Ruggiero to create a bazaar on the side of the church during the annual feast of St. Gerard. The pastor was always thinking of new ways to bring new life back into the festive celebration of St. Gerard. He was looking for a way to build a real sense of community in the parish. Father Ruggiero, contemplating the future course of the parish was concerned about the young and so he capitalized on the youthfulness of his two new young priests.

These young priests did all they could to create a new community in the ever-changing neighborhood around St. Lucy's. Father Ruggiero decided that a census would be taken of each new family who moved into the Columbus Homes, in hopes of bringing them into the life of the parish. These two young assistants filled with zeal and enthusiasm set out to work on the task that lay ahead. Father Nativo got the parishioners actively involved in the bazaar, especially the youth of the parish, the hope of the future. Little did they know or realize the role they would undertake in the very life and continuation of St. Lucy's Parish and the ever-growing annual Feast of Great St. Gerard.

During the second fifty years, we will begin to see changes in the feasts, although there were still many things that remained unchanged. Many of the traditions are still practiced but sometimes in a different way, reflecting the changes in the old neighborhood.

The Decline of the Ward and Its Anchor

"In the late 1950s, Father Ruggiero, again affirming the church as the center of the neighborhood, announced a building program which included replacing the rectory and constructing the St. Lucy's community center."[31] There was "a compelling need for a building which will provide constructive, recreational, and other facilities for all the members of the parish and residents of the community."[32] The ground breaking took place with Father Gaetano Ruggiero doing the honors, flanked by Congressman Peter Rodino, a native son of the neighborhood and of Newark. Father Ruggiero was assisted by Father Ferrechia.

In spite of the many changes in this once-thriving neighborhood, the saint still went out to greet his faithful devotees, even in the evening twilight.

As the 1950s came to a close, many of the traditions were still practiced in spite of the plight of the neighborhood and Columbus Homes looming high above our dear St. Lucy's Church and the Sanctuary of St. Gerard.

The 1960s saw the distressing decay of our dear old neighborhood. The low-income housing projects that were built, along with the rapidly decreasing population, led to the decline and deterioration of what was once Newark's thriving Italian American enclave.

What is interesting and worthy of note is that even though many familiar things were changing and collapsing, the one thing that remained unchanged and timeless in the old neighborhood was and is St. Lucy's Church and the Feast of St. Gerard. In spite of all the upheaval and unrest, St. Gerard continued to go out in procession each year to visit with his people at those old familiar stops along the procession route of the vanishing First Ward.

The Guard of Honor and the committee for the feast played an active role in the procession by manning the cart that carried the statue of St. Gerard. They also walked on each side of the cart to collect the faithful devotees' donations. Prior to the use of the cart, there is photographic evidence from as early as 1906 that a wooden carrier was used by ten to twelve men who carried St. Gerard's statue in procession throughout the streets of Newark's Fifteenth Ward, later known as the First Ward.

Anthony Pascucci, a longtime parishioner of St. Lucy's and member of the Guard of Honor, fondly recalls the use of the wooden carrier, which was recently discovered and is on display in the Newark First Ward Museum at St. Lucy's Church. Pascucci recalls:

As a child, I remember St. Gerard being carried out of the church on a wooden carrier by four members of the Church. This carrier was used until

Left: Old St. Lucy's Rectory on Seventh Avenue, circa 1950s. *Courtesy of the archives of the Museum of the "Old First Ward" of Newark, Curator, Mr. Bob Cascella.*

Below: Congressman Peter Rodino and devotees of St. Gerard. *Courtesy of the Newark Public Library M. Immerso Collection of the "Old First Ward," Charles F. Cummings New Jersey Information Center, Mr. George Hawley, Supervising Librarian.*

The Decline of the Ward and Its Anchor

St. Gerard statue carried in procession, surrounded by devotees, circa 1950s. *Courtesy of the Newark Public Library M. Immerso Collection of the "Old First Ward," Charles F. Cummings New Jersey Information Center, Mr. George Hawley, Supervising Librarian.*

the early 1950's. Three of the members I remember very well were Anthony Armellino, Rocco Rotunda and Joseph Viscido.

The first cart, which was pushed by the devotees, came in the early 1950's. I was appointed a Guard of Honor member by Reverend Gaetano Ruggiero in 1965 and was then privileged to participate in the preparation of St. Gerard from the chapel to the Main Altar where devotees came to offer their donations to him. He was carried out of the Church to the cart in front of the Church for the street procession.

In those days, we brought St. Gerard in procession to Orange St. and up to North 3rd Street and Central Avenue and returned back to the route we presently follow on Saturday. St. Gerard was processed on October 16th in the close vicinity of the Church which was 8th Avenue to Park Avenue, Mt. Prospect Avenue down to Webster Street. In those days, the procession never went beyond 2nd Avenue. In the late 1950's and very early 1960's, the procession went to North 4th Street to Christie's Restaurant, which was originally on 8th Avenue, the present site of the Colonnade Apartment parking lot.

During that time and to the present, devotees took off from work and children did not attend school on October 16th. Presently, the feast is becoming a more attended weekend feast.

The Feast of Saint Gerard Maiella, C.Ss.R.

In 1972, I was asked to help prepare St. Gerard with his new robe (habit). In attendance was Joe Viscido, taking his mother Maria's place, Clara Barone, Pasquatelle Maria Lombardi, Mr. & Mrs. Gerard Nicastro, and Vincenza. I have been asked each year since to help prepare St. Gerard with his new robe and the cleaning of the chapel.

In the early 1980's, I asked Joe Viscido if I could help with the altar flowers in St. Gerard's chapel for the Novena. I purchased the flowers with donations from my family and friends for the first part of the Novena. Joe Viscido collected money for the flower donation for the balance of the Novena and St. Gerard's feast day.

I presently take care of the altar flowers for the entire Novena along with donations from family, friends and Richard Blauvelt.

Even though many inhabitants of the "Old First Ward" moved away, they continued to return home and walk in procession as they did since they were infants, carried in procession by their parents and grandparents. Many still continue the traditions started by their ancestors and descendants. The nighttime processions continued, and so did the throngs of happy faces still waiting with fervent joy for St. Gerard to come out of church and process through the neighborhood of his people.

Mural of St. Gerard with the poor of Caposele, located in St. Gerard's Chapel. *Courtesy of the archives of the Museum of the "Old First Ward" of Newark, Curator, Mr. Bob Cascella.*

The Decline of the Ward and Its Anchor

Amidst all the turmoil, upheaval and unrest, tragedy continued to strike at St. Lucy's. The ward lost its spiritual leader and father figure when Father Gaetano Ruggiero took his final breath and went home to his eternal reward. His pastorate at St. Lucy's spanned thirty-two years. He saw many changes in his day. He led the flock through the Depression years, after the death of the saintly pastor before him, Monsignor Perotti. He even guided them through the Second World War. "His tenure spanned the First Ward's heyday as well as some of its saddest moments. While some considered him an old-style Italian Pastor, who could be at times strict and domineering, he is remembered (lovingly) by most as a kind and caring priest and a skillful administrator. He was the preeminent figure in the community for more than three decades."[33]

We certainly owe a debt of gratitude to Father Ruggiero. Thanks to his courage and foresight, the survival of the parish was secured. When he took over all the feasts at St. Lucy's, especially St. Gerard's Feast, he definitely secured the necessary income to complete the new church in all its grandeur, as well as the newly annexed Sanctuary of St. Gerard. This move on his part, difficult as it was at the time, had lasting effects that would sustain St. Lucy's during some of its most difficult times in its history. He will long be remembered as "a man of culture and wit, a man of vision and energy."[34]

This man of God loved St. Lucy's so much that he often said he would never leave St. Lucy's because that was where his heart was. When he died, he was laid out in a casket in the center aisle of the church, in front of the altar where he so often offered up the Holy Sacrifice of the Mass. The entire parish came together along with the devoted faithful of the "Old First Ward."

On Friday, February 18, 1966, a solemn high requiem mass was celebrated at 10:30 a.m. He got his wish; he was buried right on the grounds of St. Lucy's, on the side of the church near the grotto of Our Lady of Lourdes in the St. Gerard garden. Forever would Father Gaetano Ruggiero be linked with his beloved St. Lucy and St. Gerard.

Chapter 4

The Dark Days and the Pact Between the Priests and the People of the Parish

A fter the death of Father Ruggiero, St. Lucy's went through some dark days. There was a period of five years between 1966 and 1971 where there were temporary administrators who didn't understand what St. Lucy's or the Feast of St. Gerard was all about. It was during these years that Father Granato's and Father Nativo's hands were tied. They had to wait it out. Here's how Monsignor Granato explains that period in the life of St. Lucy's:

> *I'm a firm believer in Divine Providence. I truly have great faith in Divine Providence. When Father Ruggiero died, we thought we were finished then and that was in 1966. And then unfortunately, we had five years of temporary administrators who really didn't understand what this was all about. And they were very unfortunate years…Father Nativo and I were hamstrung, we couldn't say anything, and we couldn't do anything. But in 1971, I was appointed temporary administrator. And as I wrote once in our centennial memorial, an unwritten pact was made between us and the people; if you stay, we'll stay. And we both did. We all did. So we survived Father Ruggiero's death. We survived the Newark Riots. We survived Columbus Homes.*[35]

The 1999 documentary about the feast had the following to say about this time in the parish's history:

> *These were certainly challenging days for this great parish and once-thriving Italian enclave. Somehow the bond that was forged between the priests and*

The Dark Days and the Pact Between the Priests
and the People of the Parish

people assisted them in their difficult struggles and survival. In retrospect, the years that many considered to be the darkest days for St. Lucy's—1966 through 1971—may well have been its strongest years. During this time, there was unrest and turmoil in the neighborhood and throughout the City of Newark. In 1967, the city was in shambles as it was rocked by racial disturbances and riots. It was during this very difficult and painful time that the church, its people and its two young priests (Father Granato and Father Nativo) really rose to the occasion. Somehow, the two priests and the people got through this tough time together. These were St. Lucy's greatest years because with God's grace, the intercession of St. Gerard and the fierce loyalty of its parishioners, against the odds, St. Lucy's survived the storm.[36]

After Father Ruggiero's death in 1966, Jerry Spatola, a prominent Italian American funeral director and civic leader in the Italian American community, as well as chairman of the St. Gerard Feast for many years, asked his daughter Geta Spatola O'Connor to found the St. Gerard Ladies Guild. The Ladies Guild, from the very beginning, was to be dedicated to the Feast of St. Gerard and founded to promote special devotion to St. Gerard as patron of motherhood. In 1967, the guild began by celebrating St. Gerard's birthday in the month of April with a family communion breakfast. This breakfast would later evolve into an annual St. Gerard Baby Brunch beginning in 1979. This was the suggestion of Geta's son, Gerald, who became the president of the reactivated St. Gerard Men's Society after his grandfather's death.

Early on, Father Granato became involved in the St. Gerard Ladies Guild and the family communion breakfasts. At that time, he was the senior curate at St. Lucy's. From its inception in 1967 to the present, the St. Gerard Ladies Guild members played an important role in the celebration and procession of the Feast of St. Gerard.

The St. Gerard statue in procession, with Jerry Spatola to the right. *Courtesy of the Spatola family archives.*

Right: Geta Spatola O'Connor looking up at the St. Gerard statue in Materdomini, Italy. *Courtesy of the archives of Reverend Thomas D. Nicastro Jr.*

Below: St. Gerard Men's Society members. Thomas Nicastro (center) is seen carrying the society banner in procession during the feast, circa late 1970s. *Courtesy of the archives of Reverend Thomas D. Nicastro Jr.*

The Dark Days and the Pact Between the Priests
and the People of the Parish

Left: St. Gerard statue leaving St. Lucy's Church, circa 1970s. *Courtesy of the Spatola family archives.*

Below: Geta Spatola O'Connor, Thomas D. Nicastro Jr. and Gerald Spatola O'Connor at St. Gerard Brunch. *Courtesy of the archives of Reverend Thomas D. Nicastro Jr.*

St. Gerard Ladies Guild Members with guild banner outside St. Lucy's on the front steps of the church, circa late 1970s. *Courtesy of the archives of Reverend Thomas D. Nicastro Jr.*

Fathers Granato and Nativo, along with Geta Spatola O'Connor, have all played a very active role in the feast since the death of Father Ruggiero. Each in their own way has contributed of their time and energy to make this beautiful feast what it is today. Both of these priests

The Dark Days and the Pact Between the Priests
and the People of the Parish

greatly supported the work of the members of the St. Gerard Ladies Guild and Men's Society.

Another loyal supporter of the St. Gerard feast was the *Italian Tribune News*. The *Tribune* covered the Feast of St. Gerard back when the paper was still published in the Italian language. The longtime publisher of the *Italian Tribune* and a parishioner of St. Lucy's, Ace Alagna was very supportive of the church and feast. Ace always saw to it that the church and the feast were covered and highlighted in the paper, especially for significant milestones in St. Lucy's history and in the history of St. Gerard's Feast in the United States. The parish of St. Lucy's along with all the societies, guilds and clubs associated with St. Gerard's Feast are forever grateful for all the publicity given to help promote this beautiful devotion and celebration of Italian heritage and culture. This cooperation and support extends to the present day, under the present publisher, A.J. "Buddy" Fortunato, Ace's son-in-law, along with Buddy's wife, Marion Fortunato, and Joan Alagna, Ace's daughters.

Throughout the remaining years of the 1960s, the Ladies Guild continued to walk in procession and carry on the time-honored tradition passed on to them from their mothers, fathers and grandparents.

The latter part of the 1960s was a very difficult period, not only in the life of St. Lucy's parish but also in the neighborhood and the city of Newark. During these painful years, the parishioners and the priest manifested their fierce loyalty, and their camaraderie really offered hope and a beacon of light in the darkness that prevailed.

Eventually, the pain and suffering ended. The people of St. Lucy's, having experienced Good Friday in their lives for a long period of five years, would now experience the joy of Easter Sunday that would gradually unfold before their eyes through the 1970s. It was during the 1970s that many good things began to happen, and after those long painful years, the Easter flowers began to blossom again.

Commencing in 1971, Father Joseph Granato, the senior curate, was appointed temporary administrator of St. Lucy's. Now with the aid and support of his constant companion, loyal friend and brother priest, Father Joseph Nativo, they set out on a course to guide St. Lucy's back on track so that this venerable church and its beautiful Feast of St. Gerard, which unfortunately was misunderstood by some, could continue to provide this "displaced community with a space to which they can return, where the present and the past coexist against the back-drop of a living tradition."[37]

THE FEAST OF SAINT GERARD MAIELLA, C.SS.R.

Left: Priests lead the procession for the start of the walk through the old neighborhood. *Courtesy of Lisa Manderichio*

Below: Altar boys lead the procession of St. Gerard. *Courtesy of the archives of Reverend Thomas D. Nicastro Jr.*

Opposite, top: Procession of St. Gerard with the St. Gerard Ladies Guild in front. *Courtesy of the Spatola family archives.*

Opposite, bottom: In contrast, a procession from yesteryear, with Statue of St. Gerard and canopy behind with devotees following, young boys carrying candles.. *Courtesy of the Newark Public Library M. Immerso Collection of the "Old First Ward," Charles F. Cummings, New Jersey Information Center, Mr. George Hawley, Supervising Librarian.*

The Dark Days and the Pact Between the Priests and the People of the Parish

Top: Father Joseph Nativo and Father Joseph Granato walking in procession. *Courtesy of the archives of Reverend Thomas D. Nicastro Jr.*

Bottom: Altar servers lead the procession, with Father Tom Nicastro (left) and Monsignor Joseph Granato (right). *Courtesy of the archives of Reverend Thomas D. Nicastro Jr.*

During the period between the late 1960s and the early 1970s, Jerry Spatola was not only encouraging and promoting the St. Gerard Ladies Guild but also was engaged in expanding the St. Gerard Men's Society when suddenly in 1975, at the age of seventy-two, he was called to God. It was then that Jerry's grandson, Gerald Spatola O'Connor, felt called to carry on his maternal grandfather's work with the St. Gerard Men's Society. Jerry

The Dark Days and the Pact Between the Priests
and the People of the Parish

Spatola died in January 1975, and the following October, his family donated the new wrought iron cart that the statue of St. Gerard is placed on during each procession. It would replace the old cart from the 1950s. The new cart, with its covering and lights, was donated in Jerry's memory. It was first used on October 16, 1975, for his feast day. It was decorated with flowers by Pennella's Florist of Newark.

The year 1972 saw the partial closing of the twelve-story high-rise buildings (eight in total) known as the Columbus Homes. By 1990, they were boarded up and completely empty. Since 1973, St. Lucy's Parish and a few staunch parishioners (like Geta Spatola O'Connor, along with others) actively and tirelessly campaigned to get the Columbus Homes torn down forever.

After his grandfather's death in 1975, Gerald Spatola O'Connor, a fourth-generation Caposelesi descendant, reactivated the St. Gerard Men's Society. He began with a membership drive to rejuvenate the once-thriving society. The ideals of the society were to honor their patron saint and solicit funds for the feast of St. Gerard every October. The Men's Society and the Ladies Guild raised thousands of dollars for the National Shrine, as well as collected funds for the Shrine at Materdomini, the Sanctuary of St. Gerard of Maiella in the Province of Avellino, Italy.

Prior to entering the college seminary and Immaculate Conception Seminary, I became an active member of the St. Gerard Men's Society when it was reactivated in 1975. Later on, I became a trustee and worked closely with the president, Gerald Spatola O'Connor, to implement the goals, ideals and purposes of the Men's Society as a means of spreading devotion to St. Gerard, not just during the feast but also throughout the year.

Interestingly, in 1977, the St. Gerard Men's Society and Ladies Guild raised $10,000 for the feast. This goal was accomplished through the institution of a ten-week Rolling Raffle as well as through the funds collected by the Men's Society and Ladies Guild feast collection.

Members of the Circolo Progressivo Caposelesi and their Women's Auxiliary annually celebrate the Feast of St. Gerard. Each year, the club raises money in honor of its patron saint, St. Gerard. The club was originally housed on Eighth Avenue before it moved to 119 Bloomfield Avenue. This present location is now closed. The club is pretty much disbanded today, except for when it comes together for the annual Mass at St. Lucy's during St. Gerard's feast. When the club was open at its Bloomfield Avenue location, it met on the second Friday of each month at 8:30 p.m. The Circolo Progressivo Caposelesi Women's Auxiliary was organized on November 11, 1976.

Right: St. Gerard statue leaving the church for the procession, circa mid 1970s. *Courtesy of the Spatola family archives.*

Below: Gerald Spatola O'Connor (left) and Geta Spatola O'Connor (right) and photo of the late Jerry Spatola on the cape to be pinned on the statue, circa mid-1970s. *Courtesy of the archives of Reverend Thomas D. Nicastro Jr.*

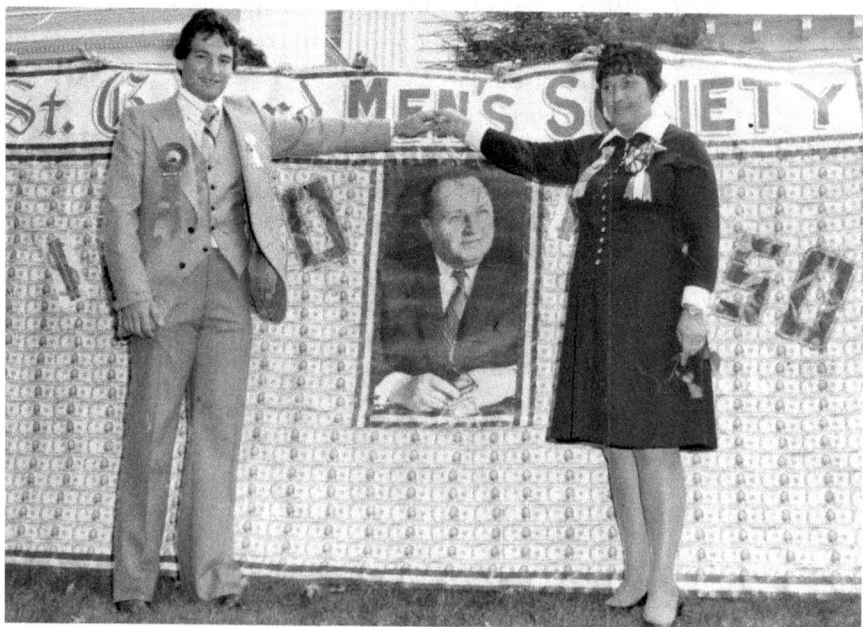

The Dark Days and the Pact Between the Priests and the People of the Parish

Men frying zeppole at the concession stand. *Courtesy of the archives of Reverend Thomas D. Nicastro Jr.*

This new cart for St. Gerard was donated in memory of Jerry Spatola by the Spatola family. *Courtesy of the archives of Reverend Thomas D. Nicastro Jr.*

Woman sitting in front of the concession stand during the feast. *Courtesy of the archives of Reverend Thomas D. Nicastro Jr.*

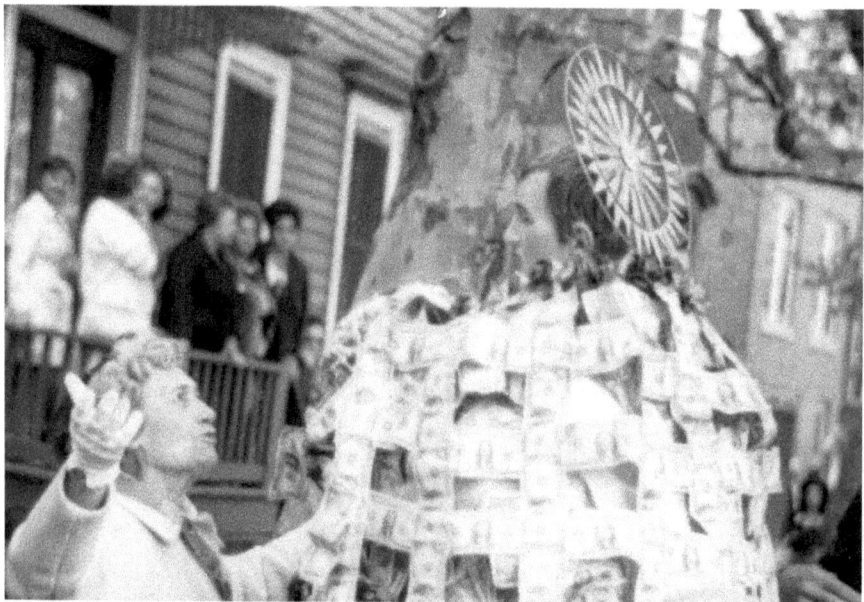

Pasquatele Maria Lombardi praying aloud to St. Gerard with great faith and devotion. *Courtesy of the archives of Reverend Thomas D. Nicastro Jr.*

The Dark Days and the Pact Between the Priests
and the People of the Parish

Annually the C.P.C. Club members and auxiliary gathered on Bloomfield Avenue and then marched in procession to St. Lucy's Church for their annual Solemn High Mass in honor of St. Gerard, a ritual instituted by the original members since its inception.

John Gonnella, a longtime devotee, was president of C.P.C. Club. Several generations of the Gonnella family have actively participated in the devotion and feast of St. Gerard. John Gonnella's father, Giuseppe Gonnella (deceased), was an original founder and first president of the St. Gerard Maiella Society back in 1920.

The fidelity of Fathers Granato and Nativo, along with the fierce loyalty of the parishioners, enabled them to forge ahead and work toward bringing to fruition the great milestones that were yet to be accomplished.

Jerry Spatola with Father Domenico Barillá, the then rector of the International Shrine of St. Gerard, Materdomini, Italy (Avellino). *Courtesy of the Spatola family archives.*

Chapter 5

The Milestone Years

The Priests, the Church and the Establishment of the National Shrine

On June 24, 1977, Reverend Domenico Barillá, rector of the Sanctuary of St. Gerard, wrote to Father Joseph Granato, Mrs. Geta Spatola O'Connor and Mr. Gerald Spatola O'Connor, stating that he received a letter dated May 16, 1977, from Archbishop Peter Gerety, announcing that he instituted at St. Lucy's Church the Confraternity of St. Gerard joined to the Arch confraternity in Italy, established by Pope Benedict XV.

Father Barillá went on to say that the establishment of this confraternity was "the most beautiful recognition of the work done by the Men's Society and Ladies Guild for almost half a century." He then went on to state that the members of the Men's Society and Ladies Guild should automatically become members of the Confraternity with the spiritual guidance of the pastor, Father Joseph Granato and his successors. He concluded by saying that each day he placed a special protection at the tomb of St. Gerard for all the activities in honor of St. Gerard in Newark and Materdomini.

On October 13, 1977, New Jersey congressman Peter W. Rodino Jr. entered St. Gerard's story and the annually celebrated feast at St. Lucy's Church into the Congressional Record of the United States of America. He called the speaker of the house's attention to a very special celebration that would he held that coming weekend in his home district. Also mentioned was the fact that the parish church would be declared a National Shrine by the then archbishop of Newark, Archbishop Peter Leo Gerety. He concluded by saying, "This weekend's feast is a time when the faithful gather together to

A wax representation of St. Gerard lying in death in a glass-covered casket in Materdomini, at the International Shrine of St. Gerard. *Courtesy of the archives of Reverend Thomas D. Nicastro Jr.*

Father Antonio, Father Luciano Panella, Geta Spatola O'Connor, Gerald Spatola O'Connor and Father Tom Nicastro during the rector's visit from Materdomini to the Newark shrine. *Courtesy of the archives of Reverend Thomas D. Nicastro Jr.*

pay tribute to the Saint whose simple humanity and unshakeable faith have given strength to our community for generations."[38]

On October 16, 1977, at the 10:00 a.m. Solemn High Mass at St. Lucy's, Archbishop Peter Leo Gerety stood in the pulpit before thousands of worshipers standing shoulder to shoulder in the aisles and pews and declared (with the full approval of the United States Conference of Catholic Bishops) that the Church of St. Lucy, the Sanctuary of St. Gerard, be henceforth called the National Shrine of St. Gerard in the United States. If that wasn't enough of a great gift in and of itself, he went one step further and made an announcement that was long awaited, one that brought tears of joy to St. Lucy's faithful staunch parishioners: he named Father Joseph Granato the pastor of the church. He had been the administrator since 1971 and now became the third pastor of the church. After the archbishop made this announcement, the faithful broke out in thunderous applause and standing ovations.

As we stop and bask in the glory and the joy of the moment now that our sanctuary, our humble shrine, was officially declared a National Shrine, we owe a debt of gratitude to Geta Spatola O'Connor and the Spatola family, starting with her grandfather Gerardo; her father, Jerry; her husband, Pat; her sister Bina; and her son Gerald, who have been actively involved for one hundred years in the feast of St. Gerard.

Beginning with the rapport established by Jerry Spatola with Father Domenico Barillá and others at the International Shrine, the groundwork was laid and the link between the shrine in Italy and Newark was solidified.

Geta Spatola O'Connor fully embraced and built upon her father's work. She invited the priests from Italy to come to St. Lucy's in Newark, as well as inviting them as guests at the St. Gerard Ladies Guild Brunch, held annually since April 1979. The priests, in particular, Father Barillá, were utterly amazed at the growth and devotion in America, particularly in Newark, where the enclave of Italians had settled years before, especially those from Caposele, Teora and the surrounding paese.

Monsignor Granato put it well in his interview from May 19, 1999. These interviews were the basis for excerpts that were used for the video produced by Steve Sefcik of Sefcik Productions for the 100th anniversary of the feast.

Really, let's be honest about it, Geta Spatola O'Connor was the one that kept suggesting this should be made a National Shrine. Then she invited Father Barillá, who was the head of the Shrine of the whole world from Materdomini in Italy, where St. Gerard is housed, where his relics are...

The Milestone Years

He came here to visit. He met with Archbishop Gerety, and then Archbishop Gerety got behind it. We had to write some letters of background, and Archbishop Gerety got the National Council of Catholic Bishops to name this a National Shrine...

Thank you, Geta, for all you did, all your hard work of love and devotion to the great wonderworker of the eighteenth century! Thank you for making our "mem'ries" so sweet and filled with joy!

Having the saint's story and the celebration of the feast entered into the Congressional Records was quite an honor, but the greatest honor that could be bestowed on St. Lucy's Church and the Sanctuary of St. Gerard was to officially declare it a National Shrine for the entire United States of America. Little did our ancestors realize what was instituted in a small, humble manner back in October 1899. And now, seventy-eight years later, it has blossomed into something so special and so great! Many, I'm sure, hoped and dreamed about this day, and surely many prayed fervently for it. Oh, how their prayers were answered!

On January 23, 1978, Archbishop Gerety presented a sculptured pewter image of St. Gerard to Reverend Joseph Granato for the National Shrine. On July 16, 1979, less than two years after the declaration of the National Shrine and being named the third pastor of St. Lucy's, a further honor was bestowed on Father Joseph Granato. He was named a monsignor by His Holiness Pope Paul VI. He became an honorary chaplain of the Papal household at the request of Newark archbishop Peter Leo Gerety.

Monsignor Granato said this honor "was bestowed more as a result of the virtue of the people of St. Lucy's rather than his own. While these sentiments reflect the humility of Monsignor, they exemplify yet again, the dynamic relationship between the people and the priest."[39]

Over the years, many people have assisted Monsignor Perotti, Father Ruggiero and Monsignor Granato in preparing for the feast. In particular, the coordinators of the feast have been invaluable in their assistance and advice to Monsignor Granato.

In my different conversations with Monsignor Granato, I asked him to share with me and reflect on some of the key people that greatly assisted him in the preparations and execution of the annual Feast of St. Gerard. He said he was very grateful for the assistance and continued cooperation of Captain Rocco (Rocky) Ferrante of the Newark Police Department, who became a good friend and loyal, faithful confidant. Monsignor said, "Anything I asked him to do, he took care of it." Monsignor explained to me

St. Gerard

Archbishop Gerety secures new status for parish shrine

By ANNE BUCKLEY

the ADVOCATE

June 2, 1977 — Page 20

NEWARK — "Around here, if you didn't know somebody's name, you could take a guess and call him Gerry, and you'd probably be right," says Rev. Joseph J. Granato, pastor of St. Lucy's. Father Granato was describing the great devotion to St. Gerard Maiella which has existed in the parish since 1899 — five years before Gerard was canonized — and which continues to increase despite the demise with the passing of the old-timers of other big devotions, ranging from St. Rocco to Our Lady of the Snows.

The devotion was brought here before the turn of the century by immigrants from Caposeli, Italy, the town where Redemptorist Father Gerard Maiello died. Those immigrants had a statue made in Italy and in 1926 built an addition to the church as the St. Gerard chapel, and now hold weekly novena devotions and an annual novena and street procession in his honor. This week the people of St. Lucy's learned of a special reward for their faithfulness: at the request of Archbishop Gerety, the confraternity of St. Gerard Maiella has been established at their parish joined to the archconfraternity established by Pope Benedict XV at the Sanctuary of St. Gerardo Maiella at Mater-domini, Italy.

Archbishop Gerety will visit that sanctuary next month and celebrate Mass in the basilica there on June 20, the day after he attends the canonization of an American, Bishop John Nepomucene Neumann also a Redemptorist.

In his May 16 letter to the rector of the sanctuary, Rev. Domenico Barilla, the archbishop asked that the confraternity be erected at St. Lucy's so that Father Granato and his successors "will be able to enroll the faithful in the confraternity and guide them in their devotion to this great saint, enabling them to gain the indulgences associated with its membership."

Archbishop Gerety had met Father Barilla last April, when the Italian priest came to concelebrate the Mass before the annual Communion-brunch which commemorates St. Gerard's birthday, April 6. Father Barilla had visited 10 years ago to say Mass for St. Gerard devotees at St. Lucy's. This time he invited Newark's archbishop to visit the original shrine.

The big celebration at St. Lucy's occurs in October, when a novena precedes the saint's feastday, Oct. 16. Literally thousands attend the observance — coming by as many as 60 buses from Rhode Island, New York State, Pennsylvania, by plane from Florida. Solid masses of people stretch for six long blocks in the street procession, through a neighborhood that has changed radically from the Italian enclave it was when the statue they follow was shipped from Italy.

The anecdote that survives from that time indicates the warmth and charm of the devotion. The little group of immigrants, gathered at the dock to pick up the statue they had ordered, had only broken English in which to make their errand known. They kept asking for Gerardo Maiella and the dockmaster kept searching the passenger list for the name.

St. Gerard has great appeal as the patron of mothers, but he is invoked for a wide variety of other favors, according to Father Granato, who is amazed at the way the devotion has grown during his 22 years at St. Lucy's. "Each year the number in the procession grows. We have letters asking for Masses and votive lights all through the year," he said. "And it is a strictly religious thing. The Mass is the high point of the feast day. The weekly novena, on Wednesday, is part of the 5:30 p.m. Mass."

Most significant is the interest on the part of the young people, Father Granato remarks. "I think it is because their petitions are being answered," he says.

Of the annual Mass and procession which draws a larger turnout every year, the priest says, "We don't exploit it, we don't promote it. We just set the dates, open the doors — and stand aside!"

Nineteenth-century immigrants imported the statue of St. Gerard Maiella from Italy for St. Lucy's Church, where it still stands, a plaster figure garbed in the fabric of a Redemptorist habit, illuminated by the flames of votive lights placed there by modern devotees.

St. Gerard article in the *Advocate*. Courtesy of the archives of the Museum of the "Old First Ward" of Newark, Curator, Mr. Bob Cascella.

that Captain Ferrante was in charge of the Emergency Division of the Police Department. During the days of the feast, he would assign approximately twelve to fourteen of his men to work the feast and assist with the security each day around the grounds at St. Lucy's, inside the church, the chapel, the rectory and the procession, and they were especially helpful with the security inside the convent when the Sister of St. John the Baptist would count the monetary donations. To borrow an expression, "He put fires out before they started." In essence, he was Monsignor Granato's right-hand man not only during the feast but throughout the year as well.

Monsignor related to me also that the trustees of the parish at the time of the feast in October served as coordinators of the feast as well. Some of the coordinators of the feast over the years included: Arsenio Saporito, Captain Rocco Ferrante, Geta Spatola, Frank Rosania, Thomas Campione, Assunta Arre, Pat Arre, Assunta's grandson and presently a Hudson County Superior Court Judge, Cosmo Alagna, Fred Buino, Louis Garruto, Anthony Pascucci, Dennis Tucci and Alan Genuario.

Emil Gianfrancisco and Philip Mercurio were in charge of securing and attending to the street vendors. Today, Alan Genuario and Joseph DeBlasio take care of the street vendors. Louis Garruto took care of the florist and garbage disposal during the feast for many years.

Anthony Rosamilia was a trustee and coordinator of the feast. He was another of the monsignor's confidants. He was highly organized and spent a lot of time in the rectory handling problems and putting out fires, so to speak. For a good number of years, he organized the security for the feast. He was assisted in this duty by Chris Imperiale, Guy Angrisani, John Warnock and James Bergamotto. He also would help out Monsignor Granato in any way he could.

Alan Genuario was always available for Monsignor Granato. When Emil Gianfrancisco and Phil Mercurio could no longer take care of organizing the vendors, Alan took over, assisted by Joseph DeBlasio. This task was a job in itself, and he undertook the task at hand in a dedicated manner. Alan is also a coordinator of the feast.

Frank Rosania was a coordinator of the feast who was highly organized and worked closely with Arsenio Saporito. During the days of the feast, he could be found in the church, the chapel and the procession, making sure everything was moving along. During the procession, he could be found directing things to make sure the procession was kept orderly and organized.

Louis Garruto was a coordinator and confidant of Monsignor Granato. When he was not walking in the procession, he could be found in the St. Gerard Plaza. He made sure the plaza was kept clean. When the St. Gerard Plaza was being built, he was Monsignor Granato's trusted advisor. He dealt with all the contractors and saw the plaza through its early stages and completion. While he was present in the plaza during the feast, he could be found greeting people and handling problems in a very calm manner. He has a very sincere, genuine devotion to St. Gerard that was instilled in him by his parents. Even from his earliest years, his mother carried him in procession.

Tom Campione was very dedicated and devoted to the church and the feast. In his quiet, laid-back manner, he watched over everything and helped in the parking lot during the feast. He also took care of the musicians and the police officers in the rectory basement during mealtime. He was always present and very loyal and had a great love for the parish of St. Lucy's.

Anthony Pascucci and Dennis Tucci were appointed coordinators of the feast by Monsignor Granato. In addition to reviewing the procession routes each year and making the necessary changes, they served as members of the Guard of Honor and assisted in coordinating the St. Gerard novena each night. They also took care of cleaning the altar candles and preparing for the next day's novena and everything that pertains to the church and chapel

THE FEAST OF SAINT GERARD MAIELLA, C.Ss.R.

Exterior of the new church with the addition of the St. Gerard Plaza after dedication.
Courtesy of the archives of the Museum of the "Old First Ward" of Newark, Curator, Mr. Bob Cascella.

of St. Gerard. Lastly, they prepare the schedules for the Guard of Honor for the novena and the feast. They give out the assignments for members to ride the cart during the procession and to assist with the distribution of the prayer cards and medals during the procession route each day.

Joseph DeBlasio is a member of the Guard of Honor. He has done a lot for Monsignor Granato behind the scenes. Prior to the procession, Joe would get St. Gerard's cart ready and make sure that it was fully functioning for that particular day's procession. After the procession, he would secure the cart until it was used again for the following procession that year. He also took care of the orange cones to block off the street or arrange them for the bus lane when buses would arrive from all over.

In years past, the Suppa Brothers provided the feast with lights. Bandstands were a part of this service, as well. Joe would employ his carpentry skills to erect the bandstand outside the front of the church.

During the course of the year, he would replace the sanctuary lights and fix the broken kneelers inside the church. He did whatever Monsignor Granato asked him to do, as well.

Rocco Ferrante Jr. used his talents and gifts for music and playing the organ as a world-renowned accomplished organist. He accompanied the St.

The Milestone Years

Lucy's Men's Choir during the feast. He played the organ for all the Solemn Masses during St. Gerard's Feast. When the statue came back to the church at night, Rocky could be found playing the traditional hymn to St. Gerard when he entered the church. He supplied the beautiful music during the benediction that followed the end of the procession.

Michele Elia was Monsignor Granato's personal secretary and parish secretary and was involved in every aspect of parish life. She handled all correspondence, donations for the St. Gerard plaza and stipends for all masses. In preparation for the feast, she typed all the letters, met with the printer, updated the list of donors to the feast and purged out dated lists from the previous year. The list could have as many as 2,300 names. She also arranged for the caterers, took care of the keys and made sure everything was ready for the beginning of the feast. Throughout the year, she took care of everything that needed to be done as a parish secretary to keep everything running smoothly. She was a loyal, faithful assistant to Monsignor Granato during his tenure as pastor.

Monsignor Granato would often say, "We would announce the Feast, open the doors and get out of the way." He believed this because, as one can see, he had many faithful, loyal, hardworking parishioners who gave 100 percent of their energy, time, talent and treasure. It was truly a joy for them to do what they did. They, each in their own way, had a great love for the parish and deep devotion to St. Gerard.

Monsignor Granato believes that most people don't come to the feast simply for a sausage sandwich, not just for the food aspect of the feast, but they come because St. Lucy's is the National Shrine of St. Gerard. They come to kneel before his statue, pleading

St. Gerard Statue in center aisle of St. Lucy's Church with clergy preparing for procession. *Left to right:* Father Tom Nicastro, Father Anthony Forte, Deacon Louis Lofreddo and a visiting priest. *Courtesy of the archives of Reverend Thomas D. Nicastro Jr.*

for favors, asking for prayers to be answered or in thanksgiving for favors received. That is why St. Gerard's feast is still going strong while other feasts died out. He is a powerful intercessor before the throne of God.

Sheriff Armando Fontoura was responsible for the security of the feast after the death of Captain Rocco Ferrante. James Bergamotto's security agency was responsible for the security of the stands and the church grounds overnight when the feast was closed. Guy Angrisani of the sheriff's department was in charge of security in the rectory and did a lot behind the scenes. Presently, John Warnock of the sheriff's department is responsible for security in the rectory during off-hours.

Each year, Anthony Pascucci and Dennis Tucci, faithful, longtime parishioners and members of the Guard of Honor, review the procession route for the feast day and other days of procession and then submit the changes and adjustments to the schedule for Monsignor Granato's approval. To this day, they both continue in the capacity.

In the old days, when Sister Celeste was alive, she and the other Sisters of St. John the Baptist ran the religious article store during the feast. Sister Celeste also employed the capable assistance of the following dedicated women of the parish to assist her in the smooth running of the religious article store and the sale of candles and raffle tickets in the St. Gerard Chapel: Micky Corbo; Frances SanGiovanni; Rose Rosania; Rose Mercurio; Jean Picone; Virginia Salerno; Gloria Hornlein; Agnes Perna; Millie Mescia; Anna Restaino, president of the St. John's Guild; and Nettie Immerso.

Sister Celeste also oversaw the counting of monetary donations at the conclusion of each of the processions. She was assisted by volunteers who gathered together in the rectory. Those who assisted her were Rose and Frank Rosania, Rose and Philip Mercurio, Mary Ann Mercurio, Micky Corbo, Connie Gesualdo, Jean Picone, Agnes Perna, Millie Mescia and Mickey and Nettie Immerso. Nettie Immerso recalled that it took up to a week to remove all the money from the capes because people stapled, taped and glued the bills to the fabric.

Jerry DelTufo coordinated the arrival and check in of the buses for the feast day and for the other days as well. He was assisted by John DiMilia.

Mr. Ralph Belangio, a member of the St. Gerard Feast Committee for many years, coordinated the list of names of the donors along the procession route. He took care of marking off the capes of money put on the saint and updating the list each year.

Sue and Anthony Pascucci took care of dividing all the medals for distribution during the feast each year.

The Milestone Years

Vito Nole was responsible for setting up the bus lanes and directing the buses after they dropped off the pilgrims each day during the feast, especially on Saturday, Sunday and whatever day the saint's feast day fell on.

Essex County executive Joseph N. DiVincenzo has always been a strong supporter of the feast and most cooperative with Monsignor Granato in giving permission and securing the necessary county permits to use county roads for the procession. He also helps in any way he can.

Through the years, the Newark Police Department and the mayor's office have been of help as well. Each year, the sheriff's department, under the direction of Sheriff Armando Fontoura, has always given their assistance and readiness to assist Monsignor Granato in all the security details to ensure that everyone who attends the feast and walks in the processions is safe. To all the police and sheriff's officers, we owe our thanks and appreciation for their loyalty over the years. Many officers have given their time and taken vacations without pay to help because of their loyalty to St. Lucy's and their faith and devotion to St. Gerard. One particular person who comes to mind is the late officer Rocco Andreotolla of the Belleville Police Department, who gave so much of his time and energy each year in protecting the faithful devotees as they came to novena each night and during the days of the feast. His loyalty and dedication will always be remembered. May he rest in peace.

The 1970s proved to be a very important milestone in the life of St. Lucy's. Certainly there was much progress in promoting St. Gerard not just locally but nationally. Because of this great interest in promoting St. Gerard as patron of mothers, babies and the unborn, the St. Gerard Men's Society and Ladies Guild directed their efforts in this area. In 1979, at the suggestion of Gerald Spatola O'Connor, president of the Men's Society, the St. Gerard April Family Communion Breakfast evolved into an annual Baby Brunch, at which new mothers were honored. At this Baby Brunch, the new mothers received the St. Gerard handkerchief and the baby relic, all of which were brought back from the International Shrine at Materdomini.

To further promote St. Gerard as the great protector of the unborn, the St. Gerard Ladies' Guild and Men's Society sponsored the new nursery wing at Columbus Hospital in Newark. Columbus Hospital, which opened its doors to the community in 1921, was originally and interestingly called St. Gerard's Hospital. The new nursery wing was dedicated in October 1982. Those present for the dedication and blessing of the new wing were Reverend Benjamin A. Piazza, pastor of St. Francis Xavier, Newark; Reverend Vincenzo Malgieri, pastor of the Church in Caposele, Italy (AV);

Geta Spatola O'Connor, president of the Ladies Guild; Gerald Spatola O'Connor, president of the Men's Society; John Magliaro, administrator of Columbus Hospital; and members and trustees of the Men's Society and Ladies Guild. This dedication was much like the other hospitals around the world that have already dedicated their maternity wards to St. Gerard.

In 1991, St. Lucy's Parish marked a great milestone in its history as the parish celebrated its centennial, one hundred years of faith and service to the people of God, the Italian immigrants and inhabitants of Newark's Little Italy, the "Old First Ward."

On March 6, 1994, three years after the 100th anniversary of St. Lucy's Parish, the long-empty and destroyed Columbus Homes that lay in ruin were torn down by implosion, to be replaced with townhouses and garden apartments. It took over twenty long, painful and stressful years to rid the once beautiful "Old First Ward" of the monstrous Columbus Homes. "After many years of being in the shadow of the ill-fated urban renewal plan that destroyed the "Old First Ward," beautiful St. Lucy's Church saw a new light a light that would shine into the future, as the feast evolved, this new light helped bring some new traditions into focus while at the same time many of the time tested traditions of the past still remained."[40]

Many former residents of the neighborhood turned out to witness the first of the buildings to come down. One week after the event, a video was shown of the implosion to several hundred parishioners of St. Lucy's. "A visibly moved Monsignor Granato told five hundred applauding parishioners, 'despite everything, you have remained loyal.' Granato attributes the 'fierce loyalty' of the First Warders to the fact that 'they didn't walk away from their neighborhood, they were thrown out.' Still, they clung to their church. 'It was their one bastion, he explains. 'It was all that was left.'"[41] According to Geta Spatola O'Connor, Monsignor Granato, Father Nativo, some of St. Lucy's parishioners and herself "leveled a campaign to get the project down after it had been condemned nationwide, it took a long time, it took a lot of perseverance and a lot of prayer."[42]

While many beautiful customs and traditions from the past remained and flourished, some new traditions came into focus that will bring St. Gerard's feast into the future as we begin the next one hundred years of this beautiful feast. After the implosion of the Columbus Homes, the feast continued to thrive as all eagerly awaited the joyful celebration of the 100th anniversary of the feast on October 16, 1999.

The love story between the "Old First Warders," their beautiful church and a saint of God and his devoted faithful continues now into the next

Above: Dedication of the nursery wing at Columbus Hospital. *Left to Right:* Reverend Vincenzo Malgieri, of Caposele; Monsignor Ben Piazza; Gerald Spatola O'Connor, president of St. Gerard Men's Society; Geta Spatola O'Connor, president of St. Gerard Ladies Guild; and John Magliaro, administrator of Columbus Hospital holding a plaque dedicating the nursery in honor of St. Gerard. *Courtesy of the Spatola family archives.*

Left: A young boy kisses the statue of St. Gerard on his cart prior to the beginning of the procession. *Courtesy of the Spatola family archives.*

Father Tom Nicastro poses for photo in St. Gerard procession. *Courtesy of Lisa Manderichio.*

century, the third millennium. Why? Because the legacy continues and is faithfully handed down from one generation to another. We must do our part then to pass on this tradition, the legacy of St. Lucy's and its beautiful feast of St. Gerard. For First Warders, their children and grandchildren, St. Lucy's Church is like no other church. It is a most sacred place where "they can reconnect with the past and live the present with a reverence for the past." A place where they can go and step back in time, if only in the pages of their minds, to feel their ancestors' presence and recall the "Old First Ward" and the Feast of St. Gerard the way it once was.

There is a feeling of warmth, comfort and joy during the celebration. It is a joining of two worlds, the old and new traditions, past and present. With joy, there is also sadness for relatives who have died since the last feast, those that are ill or women who are unable to bear children.

The devotees come before Almighty God with a profound sense of humility as they stand before him, humbly pleading their trials and tribulations. They petition the Almighty through St. Gerard, a powerful intercessor who speaks on their behalf before the throne of God. For each pilgrim, it is a spiritual journey of the mind and heart, the novena, the feast and the procession. One cannot deny the extraordinary impact of each pilgrim's personal journey and their devotion with St. Gerard.

Today, St. Lucy's Church, the hub of devotion to St. Gerard in the United States, remains, and a sprinkling of old-time faithful residents remain as well. Yes, the city's famous Little Italy has changed but not vanished from our memories, minds and hearts.

Each October 16—especially October 16, 1999, the 100th anniversary of the feast—"scattered 'Italian Americans of the 'vanished first ward' in Newark will begin their joyous return to the 'old neighborhood' for the annual feast of St. Gerard at St. Lucy's Church, with its traditional procession of the saint's 'money festooned statue' through the streets of what was once a vibrant immigrant enclave known as 'Little Italy.'"[43] Greeting the crowds will be lively band music, colorful banners and burning candles along with the aroma of a wide array of Italian delicacies such as zeppole, sausage and peppers, pizza and torrone from food vendors (bancarelle) along Ruggiero Plaza, old Sheffield Street and there in front of beautiful St. Lucy's (Santa Lucia). Dr. Constance Ferrante, in her doctoral thesis, "A Walk Through Time" (written from an anthropological perspective) stated it well when she said,

> *Certain euphoria is created as the devotees gather and revel in this collective spirit that they have engendered. Music mixes with the sounds of conversation being echoed by other devotees. On every side of the procession, one sees nothing but gestures of friendship, smiles, singing, handshakes associated with the image of the religious feast is a feeling of being welcome, a swinging open of the gates of the community so that all might enter the private world of the parish of St. Lucy to interact with boundaries of the private and public domain by the processing through the streets.*[44]

As we came together to celebrate one hundred years of faith and devotion of this feast, we focused our attention on the major component that has played an integral role in its very life. We honored the wonderworker of the eighteenth century, St. Gerard, the mothers' saint. Let us reflect for a moment on the celebration, tradition, devotion and legacy.

Saints throughout the Church's history have been associated with countries, towns, villages or even regions. For example, in the regions of Italy, there are different saints for each region or province. In the case of St. Gerard, he is the patron saint of the Campania region of Italy and the patron saint of Muro Lucano, where he was born and the town of Caposele, where he died. Saints are associated with certain problems, such as infertility or illnesses. In many parts of Italy, patron saints of various towns with their statues, processions and feasts provide people with an opportunity to express a collective identity of their devotion.

The church and the feast afford devotees of St. Gerard an opportunity to live in the present moment while still maintaining a reverence for the past. It is a spiritual renewal of their "sentimental journeys: of the mind, heart and soul with memories that are vivid and real for them." It is a celebration of "mem'ries and miracles" of the Wonderworker Saint.

Celebration is about "the spiritual and cultural observance of the feast of St. Gerard as originated and practiced by the people of St. Lucy's Church." The days surrounding the feast day are celebrated like a little Christmas or Easter not only in the bancarelle outside the church but also in the

Portrait of St. Gerard. *Courtesy of the archives of Reverend Thomas D. Nicastro Jr.*

magnificent spread of food at the devotees' homes as the saint passes by in the procession. In some cases, the concession stands are the same ones you see every year. Some families have been operating the stands for two or three generations.

Streetlights have already been a traditional part of the feast from its early beginnings (with the exception of the war years, when the lights were not on at the nighttime celebration). Elaborate arches were placed in the street. After the turn of the century, newspapers reported that the lighting display was elaborate, one seldom seen in Newark. Prior to electric lights, ten thousand oil lamps were used.

The typical celebration of the feast ranges anywhere from three to four days. The number of days that the saint goes out in procession varies from year to year depending on the calendar and how the days fall in conjunction with the Feast Day of St. Gerard on October 16. In any case, the saint always goes out on his feast day. In 1999, the celebration of the feast was a week long because of the great milestone of the 100th anniversary. That year, the saint's feast day fell on Saturday. He went in procession on Saturday, October 16, and Sunday, October 17.

Traditionally, there are specific streets that the procession covers, and certain streets are covered on the feast day itself. Even to this very day, there are certain stops on particular streets that have been covered for two or three generations. The traditional time when the procession is supposed to begin is 1:00 p.m. However, nowadays with devotees pinning their capes on the saint in church in front of the altar and outside the church, the procession doesn't always begin on time. The routes for particular days are published ahead of time each year on posters and flyers. The faithful will know in advance what day the saint will be arriving at their house. Because they have been practicing this custom every year for generations, they have a pretty good idea approximately when the saint will arrive at their family home.

Many families decorate the outside of their homes with bunting, flags and streamers, old photos of St. Gerard from Italy or statues bearing his likeness. Altars are erected with his image along with flowers and candles burning to the sound of the old familiar songs to St. Gerard in Italian. Some even decorate their homes inside as well. Years ago, when the "Old First Ward" was thriving, people's homes on the outside were elaborately decorated. Sometimes whole streets were decorated by everyone living there in order to prepare for the saint's arrival. It was a day that was second to none in the "Old First Ward" when the saint came to your street and stopped at your house. Do you remember when *nonna* and *nonno*—grandma and grandpa— prepared for the feast like no other? With all their heart and soul, they cooked, cleaned and decorated. They prepared their yard, their basement and their tables with a feast fit for a king. Why? Because St. Gerard was coming to their home! In a spiritual way, they were reconnecting with their ancestors who actually knew St. Gerard, since he lived and worked among them in the towns that surrounded Caposele, Materdomini and Teora.

Of course, when you celebrate and want to announce the arrival of someone special—in this case, a saint of God—you secure music or a band to announce his arrival. The procession could include one or two bands playing old traditional songs and hymns. In the early years, there were as many as three bands for the procession of St. Gerard. After the procession stopped along the way at the devotees' homes, they would pin their cape on St. Gerard and say their prayers fervently, in the silence of their hearts. For some, it would be an emotional display appealing to the saint of God to intercede for them for some special grace. For those few minutes, this became their sacred space and time to talk with the saint in a very real, moving way, as if the saint was still alive among them.

After their prayers, they showered the saint with flower petals and sometimes would let loose real doves in front of him. They cried, cheered, clapped and sang their songs along with the band. For an outsider to see this, they could be visibly moved to tears of joy. It was an unbelievable scene to behold!

The procession would then move on the next stop along the route. Along the way, the procession would stop at Spatola's Funeral Home, the headquarters of the St. Gerard Men's Society and Ladies' Guild. It was here that throngs gathered as they watched the Ladies' Guild and Men's Society put their annual cape on St. Gerard. Individual members would also pin their capes on at this time as well. Traditionally, Ladies' Guild president Geta Spatola

O'Connor would give out St. Gerard buttons to those in attendance. Each year, the buttons were a different, unique design. This custom of handing out St. Gerard buttons was started by Geta's father, the late Jerry Spatola.

The procession would move on from there to other stops before finally reaching the Caposelesi Club on Bloomfield Avenue. When the saint arrived at the club, which was elaborately decorated for the occasion, members would make their way atop the cart of St. Gerard to venerate him as they have done since their youth. This was a very special time for club members because it was the feast day of the patron saint of their town. St. Gerard, remember, was a tailor, and originally the members of the club were all tailors before membership was eventually opened to all Caposelesi and others.

By nightfall, the celebration really came alive with an elaborate display of fireworks letting everyone know St. Gerard was at the club. He was their special saint, and they were his people! After the stop at the C.P.C. Club, the procession headed back to the church while still stopping along the way at devotees' homes. The band continued to play. When the saint arrived back at St. Lucy's, the band played the traditional song that is always played when St. Gerard goes home to his shrine—"When the Saints Go Marching In." The fireworks would go off and the bells from the campanile rang and announced his arrival while the faithful filled the church and awaited his arrival inside. Again, it is a sight to behold to see St. Gerard bedecked with literally layers and layers of monetary capes as he is carried down the aisle while the organist plays his song and the faithful in the pews applaud.

"Tradition involves the humble beginnings of this beautiful feast and how our ancestors passed it on along with the customs that have progressed throughout the century," explained the documentary produced for the 100th anniversary. The cleaning of the statue and dressing the statue each year is a time honored custom and tradition coordinated by Joe Viscido and his wife, Theresa, for many years.

Each year, prior to the novena and feast, the statue is washed and cleaned, and Joe Viscido collects donations from the faithful to pay for a new habit, shirt and pants to be custom-made by a professional tailor. The statue is then dressed with the new Redemptorist habit and blessed in preparation for the novena and feast.

The tradition of dressing the statue in a new habit each year extends back to the old wooden church of St. Lucy. Joe Viscido relates how his late mother, Maria, and another woman by the name of Mrs. Mattia began this tradition. They decided to do so after realizing the habit on the statue was becoming worn, stained and tattered. It needed a new garment according to the specifications of the traditional habit worn by Redemptorist brothers. They then sought out a tailor to custom make a new habit for the statue.

The custom of cutting up the habit each year, along with the shirt and pants, to be given out as relics after they were blessed started after the Second World War. Joe Viscido relates how people began taking buttons off the habit and cutting small pieces of it. It was then decided to cut up the habit and vest the statue with a new one each year.

As a labor of love, Joe and his wife, Theresa, spend several hours a day for approximately a week cutting the habit and putting the pieces in little plastic bags with a blessed medal to be given out to the faithful devotees.

A new tradition has grown up around the statue before St. Gerard goes out in procession. He is prepared in his chapel with a black cape similar to the one he wore as a Redemptorist brother in Italy. After the cape is put on him and his crucifix is in place, the Guard of Honor put ribbon on both sides with straight pins so people can pin their monetary donations on him. Once the saint is prepared, he is carried by the same men each year, surrounded by the Guard of Honor.

He is lifted up and carried through the flowered arched opening decorated and donated by Al Conte of Conte's Florist. He is then brought in front of the altar in the church. At this time, devotees are lined up in the aisle of the church waiting to place their ribbon on the saint. Once this is complete, St. Gerard is ready to be brought out into procession to the sounds of bells ringing, the band playing and fireworks going off as he makes his way out of the church door to his open cart awaiting him in the street in front of the church. Since the beginning of the feast, the priests of St. Lucy's—starting with Monsignor Perotti and his associates, then Father Ruggiero and his associates and presently Monsignor Granato and his associates—walk in procession.

The earliest photograph of a priest walking in procession is of Father Ruggiero, circa 1920s. For approximately the last fifty years, Father Nativo and Father Granato have walked in procession with the saint, a tradition started in 1899 by Father Perotti. In the last several years, there have been new additions to the priestly staff that have joined in the tradition of priests at St. Lucy's walking in procession.

According to the 1999 documentary, "Bishop Nicholas DiMarzio has also been a key participant over the years. It had been a custom for him to give the novena to St. Gerard and he has returned on several occasions, by popular demand to continue this tradition." Father Anthony Granato preached at the feast day mass for many years as well, along with other priests through the years.

THE FEAST OF SAINT GERARD MAIELLA, C.Ss.R.

For over a quarter century now, I have participated in the procession in a formal way, as a priest. Prior to ordination, I was a member and trustee of the reactivated St. Gerard Men's Society in the mid 1970s. As a young child, I was brought to the feast each year by my parents and grandmothers. In 1990, I was ordained a priest and have participated in the novena (giving reflections each evening), the procession and celebration of the feast each year since then.

In order to properly celebrate the 100th anniversary, it was decided that a monument, a lasting reminder to honor our ancestors who began this beautiful tradition, should be erected on what was once Old Sheffield Street.

Interestingly, although there are only about 230 families registered in the parish, the church has a mailing list of over 2,000 names. This list of names was most helpful in the execution of a wonderful idea and plan to construct a most beautiful Italian style piazza (a plaza) in honor of great St. Gerard. In preparation for this monumental undertaking, Monsignor Joseph Granato sent out a letter dated January 15, 1999, to all the faithful devotees of St. Gerard. In his letter, he stated, "As we prepare to celebrate the 100th anniversary of the feast of St. Gerard at St. Lucy's, I write to you to urgently seek your help." He went on the say that in addition to the spiritual and social celebration, there will be a "tremendous undertaking that will require great effort, cooperation and true sacrifice." He stated that the church will be constructing a most beautiful St. Gerard Plaza with the approval and cooperation of the Archdiocese of Newark, the City of Newark and the Newark Housing Authority. The land they will be acquiring will be 83,000 square feet in front of the church. Granato said the "St. Gerard Plaza will be a fitting entrance to St. Lucy's church" and that "this Plaza will insure (*sic*) the vitality of our parish for the next 100 years." He continued by saying that the "acquisition, demolition and construction is $1,250,000.00." He then asked the faithful to make a one-time historic gift.

According to a *New York Times* article on Sunday, October 10, 1999, "the money also enabled St. Lucy's to buy a nearby warehouse owned by the Archdiocese of Newark's Mount Carmel Guild. The Newark Housing Authority agreed to split the cost of demolishing the warehouse with the church and to swap the land on which it sat for a piece of property across Ruggiero Place, the street in front of St. Lucy's, which will be rerouted around the new plaza. The intent is 'to give a welcoming feeling to an Old World Church' says its architect, Mario Barone of MJ Barone Associates in Englishtown."[45] Interestingly, Monsignor Granato stated that "...before a shovel went into the ground, we had four hundred, five hundred thousand dollars in donations on blind faith. They believed it was going to be done."[46]

114

The Milestone Years

As we move forward in the monumental task of constructing the plaza and celebrating one hundred years of faith and devotion to great St. Gerard, we not only look ahead to the bright future of St. Lucy's and St. Gerard's Feast but with warm, golden memories and nostalgia, we also look to the past and recall and celebrate the memory of our ancestors who began this devotion one hundred years ago. They never realized the impact that their faith and devotion would have on future generations to come. "We remember, we celebrate, we believe!"

Let us recall and understand that "when southern Italians began to cross the Atlantic in the 1880's, they faced the realization that they might be leaving their homeland forever. The belief in itself was a terrifying thought. The one consolation, besides the family members who accompanied them to their new land was the comfort they found in their religious beliefs."[47]

Dr. Constance Ferrante explains the importance of religion and church for the tight knit immigrant community in a strange new world. She stated, "Religion, as a vehicle by which the immigrants were able to continue their beliefs, provided a comfortable liaison between Europe and the United States. In essence, religious beliefs and their differing modes of expression provide continuity to the community, especially to immigrants."[48] For the immigrant Italian Catholic, the church, customs and traditions went hand in hand. The church became a place of security for the insecure immigrant in a strange new land and a comfortable means to practice their faith in the context of familiar surroundings with others of the same ethnic background. "Many devout Italians, however, perceived these customs to be essential to worship and to the maintenance of tradition."[49] Ferrante goes on to say, "For Catholics, life in the immigrant community centered around the Catholic parish, both the parish and the immigrant community served as a means by which part of the old world was transplanted into the new."[50]

Having reflected on the immigrant experience of the importance of religion, the church and the tight-knit immigrant community, one can truly see how the Catholic parish and the Catholic experience became ingrained in the lives of that humble band of Caposelesi immigrants in 1899. Little did our ancestors realize that what they did became the impetus for transplanting old world customs and outward demonstrative expressions of devotion to the saints, not only in the new world but also for generations to come. This devotion to St. Gerard has been passed on as a timeless custom that is fully alive in the twenty-first century at St. Lucy's in Newark and beyond.

Believe it or not, one hundred years have passed since that first band of Caposelesi came together with a simple picture of a humble lay brother (commonly known today as a co-adjuter brother) of the Congregation of the Most Holy Redeemer.

The milestone had arrived, and a series of events leading up to the centennial celebration of the Feast of St. Gerard were about to unfold.

Prior to the 100th anniversary celebration and in connection with the Feast of St. Gerard and St. Lucy's Church, a project was started in 1994 and finished in 1996 by Newark native Michael Immerso. It chronicled the Italian American experience in Newark's Little Italy, the vanished First Ward. The project was dedicated to preserving the neighborhood's experience in what was once the fifth-largest Little Italy in the United States. An exhibition was held at the Newark Public Library, where a permanent archive was set up to preserve the Italian Immigrant experience in old photographs that were collected from as far away as Florida, Texas and California. In addition to this exhibition, there was published a companion book with photos and stories by Rutgers University Press in June 1996.

On June 19, 1997, there was a reception and screening of a companion documentary on "Newark's Little Italy: The Vanished First Ward." The video was narrated by Steve Adubato Jr. of Caucus Educational Corporation. The event was held at the North Ward Center, Inc., under the direction of Stephen N. Adubato Sr., executive director. This screening was presented by the Caucus Educational Corporation in association with the Newark Public Library.

As one can see from the exhibition at the library, as well as the book and the video, St. Lucy's Church and the Feast of St. Gerard is the center and the hub of the Italian American experience in the old neighborhood—once thriving, now vanished—forever etched in our minds, hearts and memories.

The most significant event was the adopting of a resolution on December 2, 1998, by the City of Newark's Municipal Council to support St. Lucy's Church in celebrating the 100th anniversary of the Feast of St. Gerard to be held in Newark's "Old First Ward" on October 16, 1999. The resolution further encouraged "the city of Newark's institutions and agencies to acknowledge and celebrate this historical and cultural landmark event." The resolution was signed by the president of the council and by Robert P. Morasco, the city clerk. On December 21, 1998, the city clerk sent a letter to Monsignor Joseph Granato concerning the adoption of the resolution and the full support of the City of Newark with the institutions and agencies to celebrate the centennial celebration. In recognition of this significant milestone and in connection with Immerso's book and Adubato's documentary, the Nevarca Project was born. The full title of the project was

The Milestone Years

"Nevarca, Celebrating the Italian Experience in Newark." The word *Nevarca* is "an Italian transliteration of Newark often used by Italians to address friends in the immigrant community of Newark, New Jersey."[51]

The Nevarca Project was chaired by Michael Immerso. The participating institutions are listed as follows:

> *The Newark Public Library, The Newark Museum, New Jersey Performing Arts Center, New Jersey Historical Society, Joseph and Geraldine C. LaMotta Chair in Italian Studies at Seton Hall University, Rutgers Institute on Ethnicity, Culture and the Modern Experience, St. Lucy's Church, The North Ward Center, Inc., The Center for Italian and Italian American Culture, Inc., the Italian Tribune, Archdiocese of Newark, the Vice Consulate of Italy, Columbus Hospital, New Jersey State Opera, National Italian American Foundation, Newark Preservation and Landmarks Committee, the Office of the Mayor and The Newark Municipal Council.*

The goal of the project is defined in a packet that was mailed to many people in the community and throughout the state.

> *The focus of Nevarca: A Celebration of the Italian Experience in Newark in anchored around the celebration of the centennial anniversary of the feast of St. Gerard in Newark. (Nevarca is the transliteration of Newark.) The feast of St. Gerard is an enduring expression of Italian tradition in Newark spanning an entire century and provides a unique opportunity to celebrate the City's cultural legacy and its ethnic heritage. This centennial is a significant historical and cultural landmark for the City of Newark and its surrounding communities.*[52]

Michael Immerso continues with his explanation of the Nevarca Project:

> *the project will explore the role of Newark's immigrants from both a social, historical and artistic perspective. Programs to take place city-wide will include: studies on art and architecture, the community's political impact; and discussions on culture and ethnicity, including the history of Italian women in America and the role of religion in Italian culture...Perhaps more than any other Italian-American institution, the Feast of St. Gerard at Saint Lucy's Church has evolved into an Italian-American cultural and spiritual landmark recalling the immigrant aspirations of Newark's earliest*

THE FEAST OF SAINT GERARD MAIELLA, C.Ss.R.

Italian settlers, drawing together Italian-Americans from all corners of New Jersey who share a common link with the city.[53]

On September 30, 1999, from 6:00 to 8:00 p.m., the Nevarca Project commenced with a cocktail reception at the North Ward Center, Inc, Newark. This milestone event celebrated the centennial celebration of the Feast of St. Gerard with a series of events lasting one month. The gala included a reception with refreshments, speakers and Italian music. Attendance was by invitation only. The following dates and events are taken from a brochure and poster prepared by Neverca Project chairman Michael Immerso.

October 2–3, 1999, the Nevarca project sponsored a workshop, "Buildings Have a Story," exploring the history of St. Lucy's in Newark.

From October 4, 1999 thru December 31, 1999 there was an exposition of photographs "documenting and interpreting the Italian-American Legacy in Newark." This exhibition was held at the Newark Public Library.

October 6, 1999 from 12:15 to 1:00 p.m. "Stories in Glass"

October 7, 1999–October 15, 1999
"The Nightly Novena" honoring great St. Gerard. This includes the "blessing of newborns and blessing of expectant mothers." The novena is held at St. Lucy's, the National Shrine of St. Gerard in the United States.

October 8, 1999
National Landmark Ceremony
"Newark Preservatory and Landmarks Committee ceremony designating Saint Lucy's Church a national landmark."

October 9, 1999
Workshop: Glowing Colors
"Celebrating St. Lucy's Church; "Children will draw, color and create a stained glass window."

An article appeared in the *New York Times* on the 100th anniversary of the Feast of St. Gerard. St. Lucy's Church celebrated the centennial of the Feast with a Dinner Dance on October 10, 1999 at the Birchwood Manor, Whippany, New Jersey.

The Milestone Years

An ad book was being put together to celebrate this event that was printed for the dinner dance. In promoting the journal to commemorate this special event, Monsignor Granato wrote in a letter for the 100th Anniversary of the Feast of St. Gerard,"…in thanksgiving for his many favors, the devotees of St. Gerard are working hard and diligently to make this celebration of his Centennial Feast a special tribute of gratitude for his continual help. We are creating a commemorative Ad Book for this blessed and happy occasion. Your support will lend needed assistance in the preservation of the National Shrine of St. Gerard at St. Lucy's Church."

One of the special highlights of the 100th anniversary dinner dance was the viewing of a very special project that was completed in time for the centennial celebration. An hour-long video that documented the first one hundred years of the history of the feast of St. Gerard played for all in attendance. The committee continuously ran the video, which took viewers back to the early beginnings of the feast and the story of the Caposelesi community that fostered this devotion to Brother Gerard Maiella C.S s.R., saint of heaven and earth. The video documentary was on sale for the upcoming feast. The professional company that produced the video was Sefcik Productions.

The executive producer was Gary Genuario, a parishioner of St. Lucy's. The original story of the history of the feast was researched and written by Reverend Thomas D. Nicastro Jr. The screenplay was written by Gerard Nazzareto, Reverend Thomas D. Nicastro Jr. and Gary Genuario. The members of the committee for the video documentary production were: Gary Genuario, Reverend Thomas Nicastro, Geta Spatola O'Connor, Gerald O'Connor, Gerard Nazzareto, Dennis Tucci, Anthony Passucci and Michelle Dalbo.

The interviewees included: Reverend Monsignor Joseph J. Granato, Geta Spatola O'Connor, Frank Rosania, Joseph Viscido, Dr. Constance Ferrante, Michelle Dalbo, Mary Jo and Gerald Melillo, Connie Amato DeMeo, Arsenio Saporito, Lou Garruto, Michael Immerso, Reverend Thomas Nicastro, Gerald O'Connor, Joseph Gonnella, Anthony Coppola, Angela and Raymond Salerno, Margaret and John DeCorso, Mina Yannuzzi, Connie DiGennaro, James Restaino, Sister Frances Marie and Madeline Verlingo.

The video documentary consisted of the spoken history of the feast by a professional narrator and featured old photographs, film footage and videotaped interviews of people who had some connection with the feast over the last one hundred years. Some of those who participated in the interviews were the direct descendants of those members of the Caposelesi colony who started the feast in 1899. This documentary is truly a gift and a great treasure for those who participate in the feast annually and are active members of St. Lucy's Church. Since the production of the video, many key participants have gone to their eternal reward or are no longer able to communicate the wealth of knowledge they so freely and lovingly gave to the committee for the sake of posterity, passing on to future generations what transpired in these precious one hundred years. Thank God the video was completed when it was. Now we have a lasting treasure that could never have been produced without all the key participants.

Another lasting treasure put together for the 100th anniversary was a book entitled *Memories and Miracles*, under the direction, guidance and supervision of the late beloved associate pastor of St. Lucy's, Reverend Joseph Nativo. For approximately forty-eight years, he served at St. Lucy's and worked side-by-side as the faithful, loyal friend and associate of Monsignor Joseph J. Granato. This book contains many letters and testimonies from devotees of St. Gerard from near and far and a biography of St. Gerard, which speaks of the special favors and blessings bestowed on his devoted friends. There is a brief account of the origins of the feast as well as beautiful pictures. It is truly a keepsake for all the family for generations to come.

THE EVENTS SURROUNDING 100TH ANNIVERSARY CONTINUE

October 13, 1999
Photography and Ethnicity (12:15–1:00 p.m.)
Photographer, John Matturri, using his series of photographs of the feast of St. Gerard will lead a discussion of the celebration, the community and the nature of photography."

October 13, 1999
Big Night (5:30–7:30 p.m.)
Screening of Stanly Tucci's endearing film about two Italian brothers.

October 16–17, 1999
Feast of St. Gerard (100th Anniversary)
Daily Processions with the Statue of St. Gerard. The program of October 16, 1999 will include the formal dedication of the St. Gerard Plaza.

The Milestone Years

October 20, 1999
Painted Memories (12:15–1:00 p.m.)
Artist Maria Cicchino traces elements in her work to visits to Italy and memories of Italian life.
October 27, 1999
Lasting Impressions in Print (12:15–1:00 p.m.)
Susan Boynton, local printmaker spent 12 years working in Italy.

October 29, 1999
An Italian Saint and his community, St.Gerard Maiella and Newark's First Ward (3:00–5:30 p.m.)
A symposium hosted by the Joseph M. and Geraldine C. LaMotta Chair in Italian studies at Seton Hall University. Speakers include Prof. Rudolph M. Bell; Prof. William J. Connell; Dr. Constance Ferrante; Michael Immerso; Prof. Elizabeth Milliken; Father Thomas D. Nicastro, Jr.; Father Lawrence Porter; Peter Savastano. To be followed by a reception and presentation of the First Annual Italian Culture Medal. Seton Hall University, Kozlowsky Auditorium, Kozlowsky Hall, 400 South Orange Avenue, South Orange, 973-275-2928.

October 30, 1999
The Italians of Newark Spirit and Memory, Past and Present (10:00am–1:00pm)
A symposium hosted by the culture and the modern experience celebrating a Century of Italian American history and memory in the City of Newark. Keynote Speaker: Professor Rudolph J. Vecoli, University of Minnesota. The program will include memories and recollections from a cross section of Newark's Italian American community and a special screening of the documentary film Newark's Little Italy: The Vanished First Ward. *Rutgers University, Paul Robeson Campus Center, 350 Martin Luther King Jr. Blvd., Newark, 973-353-5410"*

—Michael Immerso, chairman, from a flyer from the "Nevarca Project Celebrating the Italian Experience in Newark."

The highlight of the centennial celebration was the concelebrated Mass of Thanksgiving. The principal celebrant was Most Reverend Theodore McCarrick, Archbishop of Newark, now Theodore Cardinal McCarrick, Archbishop Emeritus of Washington. The concelebrants of the mass

Archbishop Theodore McCarrick blessing the St. Gerard statue in the new St. Gerard Plaza for the 100th anniversary of the feast as Monsignor Granato looks on. *Courtesy of Lisa Manderichio.*

included the Most Reverend Nicholas Di Marzio; Monsignor Joseph Granato; his associates, Reverend Joseph Nativo and Reverend Anthony Forte. The other priests concelebrating were Reverend Anthony Granato; Reverend Thomas D. Nicastro and Reverend Joseph Ambrosio.

The concelebrated Mass of Thanksgiving began at 12:30 p.m. in honor of our beloved saint. The mass was given by the members of the St. Gerard Ladies Guild and the St. Gerard Men's Society. The 11:00 a.m. mass was celebrated by Bishop Nicholas DiMarzio.

At the conclusion of the Solemn High Concelebrated Mass of Thanksgiving at 12:30 p.m., the altar servers lead the priests, the pastor and the archbishop outside for the formal dedication and blessing of the beautiful new St. Gerard Plaza. Although not fully completed, the plaza was bedecked with beautiful, bright floral arrangements. The archbishop formally dedicated and blessed the new St. Gerard Plaza in the presence of the priests, the politicians and throngs of devoted faithful who looked on with great joy, pride in their hearts and a real sense of nostalgia.

As I stood there with tears of joy, I looked around at those present, young and old and thought about those yet to be born in their mother's womb. I then thought back to yesteryear when on that very same spot, on old Sheffield Street, the "Old First Ward" was an enclave of Italian immigrants who began this beautiful tradition with the saintly first pastor, Monsignor Joseph Perotti. What was interesting and endearing was the fact that many of those who started this feast in a humble way on October 16, 1899, one hundred years ago and who walked in those first processions were now today represented by the next generation. I know first-hand, since my grandparents walked in procession faithfully each year since their arrival from the old country.

Oh, the joy they must feel in heaven as they all looked down on their families, their great-grandchildren and grandchildren. We truly owe a debt

Archbishop Theodore McCarrick blesses and dedicates the new St. Gerard Plaza with Monsignor Granato to the left and Father Anthony Forte to the right. (100th Anniversary of the St. Gerard Feast.) *Courtesy of Lisa Manderichio.*

Monsignor Joseph Granato with Archbishop McCarrick and politicians at the dedication of the St. Gerard Plaza during the 100th anniversary of the feast. *Courtesy of Lisa Manderichio.*

THE FEAST OF SAINT GERARD MAIELLA, C.Ss.R.

Monsignor Joseph Granato and Father Tom Nicastro pose for a photo during the procession. *Courtesy of the archives of Reverend Thomas D. Nicastro, Jr.*

of gratitude to their faith, devotion and fierce loyalty to *La Chiesa di Santa Lucia, Santuario di San Gerardo Maiella*, the Church of St. Lucy, the Sanctuary of St. Gerard Maiella in America.

In preparation for the centennial celebration, the *Italian Tribune News* ran a front-page article on the 100th anniversary of the feast with the entire centerfold dedicated to the history of the feast in photos and a corresponding story. In the September 16, 1999 edition, Paul Rosetti wrote concerning the plaza, "Father Granato, who thanks the Housing Authority for the land and the City of Newark and the Mayor's office for their help, reports that the Plaza comprises of 83,000 square feet in front of St. Lucy's. The statue of Saint Gerard will be placed on a wall which will be four feet high and eighty feet long and have the names of devotees engraved upon it."

All of the beautiful statues placed in the new plaza were crafted in Italy and made from Carrera marble. Towering high above the statue of St. Gerard is a beautiful statue of the Blessed Mother overlooking the church. Some of the other statues include St. Joseph, St. Anthony, St. Pio of Pietrelcina and Father Fusco, the founder of the Sisters of St. John the Baptist. Another prominent statue is the Sacred Heart of Jesus, which

The St. Gerard statue, made of Carrera marble, in the plaza. *Courtesy of Lisa Manderichio.*

overlooks the City of Newark and welcomes pilgrims to the National Shrine with open arms. Included as well in this peaceful oasis in the heart of the City of Newark are the Stations of the Cross, the Mysteries of the Rosary and a life-size crucifix on the opposite side of St. Joseph. St. Joseph faces Seventh Avenue and the crucifix faces the church.

Truly, this beautiful St. Gerard Plaza, constructed under Monsignor Granato's leadership and the assistance of Mr. Louis A. Garruto, chairman of the St. Gerard Plaza Campaign, along with the support, help and financial assistance of the faithful, honors our ancestors who started St. Lucy's greatest tradition, the Feast of St. Gerard. It will be a vivid and lasting reminder for generations to come of this once great neighborhood.

I believe the rebirth has taken place, and now St. Lucy's and the Feast of St. Gerard can securely move into the twenty-first century so that this great tradition and legacy will not only be passed on but can also be connected with the hopes and dreams of those gone before us. Our beautiful St. Gerard Plaza truly acts as a serene and peaceful barrier that guards and protects the church as a spiritual oasis in the midst of a changing neighborhood. It is a place to experience a little bit of heaven on earth, since it leads into the sacred and hallowed walls of St. Lucy's, known as the "Italian Cathedral."

As I draw to a close the glorious history of this feast and its parish, recall our "grandmother's treasure," which is our heritage and legacy. It has been placed in our hands just like the treasure that the daughter of Angelo Pirofalo placed in her grandson's hands, the remains of St. Gerard's handkerchief, the devotion to the patron of mothers and their unborn children. Remember that this treasure has become our heritage. The legacy must be passed onto the next generation. Now, as we look to what some might say is an uncertain future, recall the words of Monsignor Joseph Granato, third pastor of St. Lucy's, "I believe all you have to do is keep doing what we've been doing…

Miracolosa Immagine
di
San Gerardo Maiella
Venerata nel Santuario Omonimo nella
Chiesa di Santa Lucia
Newark, N. J.

Old postcard of the St. Gerard statue.
Courtesy of the archives of Reverend Thomas D. Nicastro Jr.

The devotion is here, nothing will change that. It just has to be protected and guided, that's all."

Devotees of great St. Gerard, remember as in the past that Divine Providence has always provided for you and your beautiful church. Mary, the mother of God has wrapped her mantle around this sacred place. Your powerful friend and helper has never failed you and will always watch over and protect St. Lucy's and this beautiful feast. All you have to do is make a pilgrimage here, kneel before him after you first visit our Divine Lord in the Blessed Sacrament, where he is really and truly present. Then light your candle, whisper your prayer to Brother Gerard and remind him of what he said so long ago to his friend and confrere—"and would I forget you?" St. Gerard will not forget us. God will provide for the future of this very special place and special feast. Remember to pray for the needs of this parish, the changing neighborhood and the city, the needs of the National Shrine and for the official recognition of St. Gerard as patron of mothers and their unborn children, as well as for the placement of St. Gerard on the liturgical calendar in the United States for October 16, his feast day.

Chapter 6
The Treasure and the Heritage Continues

The Legacy of St. Gerard Maiella's Feast

We would be remiss if we did not mention the "marvelous privilege which God seemed to have imparted to our saint, namely that of protecting mothers and children in the numerous dangers that accompany maternity. There are some countries where there is not a mother who has not his picture and who does not devoutly invoke his name."[54]

This great gift and privilege given to St. Gerard was even manifested in his holy but very short lifetime. Many today, as in the past, who have invoked his help and intercession are very grateful and have begun a tradition of naming their little ones after this great saint who has become their heavenly patron and protector even while still in their mother's womb.

There are many wonderful stories about the wonder of St. Gerard, and here are just a few. There was a woman in the town of Senerchia who was in a desperate state of illness and about to die. Her friends had recourse to Gerard. He promised to pray for her. No sooner had he prayed, their sorrow was changed to great joy.

Then there is the famous handkerchief story about the young daughter of Angelo Pirofalo. Gerard one day dropped his handkerchief on a chair in the house as he was leaving. The young girl hurried to him to give him back this treasured gift he left. He told her to keep it, saying, "It will be useful to you some day." Years later, she had married and was at the point of dying while carrying her first child; she remembered the holy brother's famous last words and called for the handkerchief of his which was in safekeeping. As soon as she applied it to her womb, both she and her child survived the near fatal ordeal because of the power of St. Gerard's handkerchief. The danger passed quickly, and now that heavenly handkerchief stands as a symbol of hope for those having difficulty conceiving and for mothers expecting a child.

Another example was a child who was born in Oliveto. He died immediately after the saving waters of baptism were poured over him. Gerard's powerful assistance was implored immediately by the parents, Tommaso Ronco and his wife. They immediately applied his relics to their lifeless child. Upon application of his relics, the child began to breathe again. The baby's life was saved thanks to the heavenly helper of mothers and their children. "The renown of the numberless prodigies operated by the servant of God has so roused the confidence of the people, that it surpasses all belief. He is everywhere invoked, his picture is asked for everywhere, and everywhere are instances of his marvelous protection related."[55]

The beautiful custom of parents naming their children after this great heavenly protector goes all the way back to his lifetime. Even before he passed into heavenly glory to take his place as one of God's great heroes in the harvest of saints, he was watching over the unborn and encouraging their parents as their great champion, the champion of life.

During the summertime of 1754, the year before he died, his friend and *paesano* (fellow townsman) Alessandro Piccolo, who had married a second time, paid Brother Gerard a visit at the Convent of Materdomini. Listen now to what transpired in their conversation. Gerard spoke these words to Alessandro, "Live in contentment and with a good heart with your wife. She is forty days pregnant and will give birth to a boy." It all rang true, what Gerard had prophesied. "Master Alessandro esteemed Gerard so greatly that he wished to give the boy that same name even before he was born. The most amazing thing was that every time the father placed his hand over the belly of his wife and said 'Gerardo, Gerardo,' he felt the baby move within the womb of his mother and pound at the place of his hand."[56]

Little did Alessandro Piccolo of Muro Lucano realize that what he was doing in the summer of 1754 would grow into a worldwide custom of naming children after this great heavenly protector of theirs.

It is truly amazing that for over two hundred years our treasured saint has assisted those couples in need, especially those having difficulty with conception. Many have testified that he was the specialist to see and came to the rescue of those in danger of losing their precious child in the womb. These are the traditions begun in the eighteenth century while Brother Gerard was still alive, traditions that have reached down from then until now.

Devotees of St. Gerard, we are the keepers of these beautiful traditions concerning Brother Gerard's love for human life, especially for the unborn in their mothers' wombs and for mothers and fathers themselves. When you stop and think about it, we are part of an unbroken chain, a link to what took place in the eighteenth century. How many countless husbands and wives name their children after Brother Gerard because of their great love and respect for him and his great concern for the unborn child?

Now is a good time to stop and reflect. Did not our ancestors come in frequent contact with Brother Gerard Maiella, who lived and worked among them?

Brother Gerard was truly the saint of the people. He never refused to help those who came to him in need. He was always praying for them, advising them, guiding them, writing letters to them and performing miracles to meet requests or needs of the people. Gerard "was the pilgrim who crossed the fields, met the peasants, spoke to workers in his and their coarse rustic dialect."[57]

As we celebrate and recall this saint's holy life, we are charged to pass on these traditions to our children. Parents instill in them this great love and trust for our eighteenth-century wonderworker and friend! As we continue to carry on these traditions and celebrations, we are securing the legacy. All of these things combine to make the Feast of St. Gerard a sacred and timeless ritual of faith and devotion.

I feel blessed to share with you the pearls of wisdom of St. Gerard, one of the rarest and brightest stars to shine in heaven and one of the greatest saints in the Catholic Church that I have come to know and love.

"No tomb," states Father Carr, "is deep and dark enough to imprison the memory of a saint or quench his light. Gerard had even been regarded as a walking saint on earth no sooner had he left it than he was looked upon and invoked as a glorified saint in heaven."[58]

Thursday, October 16, 1755, saw the passing of a great saint.

> *But the saints do not pass. They do indeed pass out from the sight of their generation, but only to return after a longer or shorter period, arrayed in all the might and splendor of their canonized holiness, to live again in the minds and hearts of generations unending that have never known them in the flesh and that now give them a reverential love and turn to good account their powerful meditation with Heaven. There is surely something not of this world, something eternal in the Church's undying remembrance of her saintly dead.*[59]

As I look back and reflect over these last one hundred years, I think back to my many trips to the International Shrine at Materdomini and recall all the pilgrims who came and who continue to come to visit the great wonderworker of the eighteenth century. Today, they come by modern means of transportation. I think back to my ancestors and the stories told to me by my maternal grandmother of how they walked all day in pilgrimage with other children and families from their little town of Teora. Now fast-forward to the twenty-first century, when I watch the many busloads of pilgrims who come each year to the National Shrine in Newark. In all of this, there is definitely a common thread in the expression of this devotion. They come with their simple faith and devotion and for a favor for themselves or a loved one. They light their candle, pin their donation on him and pray with great faith.

It is truly a love story between the people who came here from Italy and their powerful friend and helper, Brother Gerardo Maiella, a love story of the inhabitants of Newark's "Old First Ward." We all have our stories and histories with St. Gerard. Today, we come here no longer to a tiny wooden church, but to a magnificent church we call the Italian Cathedral, St. Gerard's true home in America. Buses filled with pilgrims come hoping, praying, crying, asking for some help, some relief, some small miracle or favor as they always have since he lived and walked among their ancestors in Italy.

As we go in pilgrimage once again, remember it is a good time to recall the words tradition, celebration, devotion and legacy!

This sacred space and place we call St. Lucy's is filled with memories, memories for me that are so powerful that these very hallowed walls cry out on high holy days like these. This is the spiritual home of our ancestors; this is our home, our church and our shrine that has become sanctified by years of devotion, customs and rituals that will never die.

Recently, as I looked at old photographs, I thought about the wonderful connection and bond the people of St. Lucy's shared, not only with St. Gerard and the other saints here, but the special and treasured bond between the parishioners, the priests of St. Lucy's and Newark's "Old First Ward."

When we look back and reflect on the history of this beautiful feast, I realized that from the very beginning of the history of this church and especially the Feast of St. Gerard, the Good Lord always gave St. Lucy's and St. Gerard priests who genuinely loved and cared for the flock and who sacrificed greatly for the good of the parish and this great feast. For that alone, we should give thanks to God and remember priests like the first pastor, the saintly Monsignor Perotti; the strong and wise spiritual leader, Father Gaetano Ruggiero, who saved this feast and protected the financial best interest of the church; the warm, lovable and approachable Father Joseph Nativo; and the humble, prayerful third pastor, Monsignor Joseph Granato, who places great faith in Divine Providence. He, along with his friend and partner Father Nativo, have guided St. Lucy's parishioners and the Feast of St. Gerard through some dark, stormy days. Monsignor Granato has sacrificed his time, energy and life here at St. Lucy's for over fifty years.

When you think back to its humble beginnings, these priests have served, sacrificed and remained loyal and faithful to the parishioners of St. Lucy's. They have been your rock of support for over one hundred years. That's incredible!

The Treasure and the Heritage Continues

As you walk through this sacred place and space and visit great St. Gerard, leave with the memories, traditions and customs of your parents and grandparents and pass them on to your children as you walk again outside to celebrate the annual Feast of St. Gerard. As you turn back the pages in your mind, recall this magical time of the year when the "Old First Ward" comes to life and for a brief moment you see, feel and recall with great emotion the presence of your deceased loved ones. if for only a brief shining moment. In his work on the "Old First Ward," Michael Immerso said, "It is easy for a moment to let the intervening years to fade from memory and to imagine the old neighborhood still thriving and alive outside the church doors."[60]

What my grandmother and many other grandmothers have left us is a rich and powerful legacy for many years to come. We must do our part then to carry on this living, loving tradition by continuing to spread devotion to St. Gerard all over the world. This legacy that as been handed on to us and entrusted to us is beautifully expressed in a poem I read in *Chicken Soup for the Soul*, by Jack Canfield and Mark Victor Hansen. The poem, whose author is unknown, goes like this:

The Legacy

When I die, give what is left of me to children. If you need to cry, cry for your brothers (sisters) walking beside you. Put your arms around anyone and give them what you need to give to me. I want to leave you with something, something better than words or sounds. Look for me in the people I have known and loved. And if you cannot live without me, then let me live on in your eyes, your mind, and your acts of kindness. You can love me most by letting hands touch hands and letting go of children that need to be free. Love does not die, people do. So when all that is left of me is love...give me away...

The words of this beautiful poem speak to me about the rich and powerful legacy our grandparents and parents have handed on to us concerning our devotion to St. Gerard. Our memory is our most precious ability to recall past events. Remember those many times we walked with our relatives in procession asking for a favor, hoping for some miracle from this great wonderworker. How many times did that familiar cart bearing his image come by your house? What about the many times he blessed you and your loved ones? As we celebrate one hundred years of faith and devotion, listen carefully as you walk in procession. Permit yourself to step back in time and feel your parents and grandparents presence, listen to the words and sounds on their lips as they prayed those beautiful prayers in their native tongue, feel their presence as you listen to the band play those old familiar pieces as they

Newly restored statue of St. Gerard. His arms and hands are now positioned the way they originally were when he first came to us. *Courtesy of the archives of Mr. and Mrs. Joseph DeBlasio.*

stop at your house as he with his eyes lifted toward heaven passes by. Then, when you realize that you've only stepped back in time in the pages of your mind, "put your arms around (your brothers and sisters) and give them what you need to give to (your deceased loved ones.)"

Realize that what "(they) wanted to leave you and me was something better than sounds or words." They wanted to hand on to us this rich and powerful legacy of faith and devotion to St. Gerard. Look for them and you will see them in all "the people (they) have known and loved." "And if you cannot live without (them), then let (them) live on in your eyes, your mind and your acts of kindness." Let them live on in this living, loving tradition that you and I must carry on into the next generation. Remember that their "love" for you and me and this tradition "will not die, for only people do" "so when all that is left of (them) is love give (them) away."

Before you take leave of them and this joyful celebration of one hundred years, walk again through the doors of that old familiar church; experience the sacredness of those hallowed walls of that peaceful sanctuary where he still stands so humble and tall waiting for you and me to come and talk with him about the problems and the fears that weigh upon our souls. Then, so gently, he will lead you and me to Christ, a prisoner in the tabernacle, as he so often said, a prisoner waiting there for you and me to bring us grace and peace, true and lasting joy.

Oh, Great St. Gerard, wonderworker of the eighteenth century, hear our plea and answer our prayers, if it be God's holy will. Watch over, protect and bless our beloved St. Lucy's, your National Shrine in America.

"Saint of the Mountain"

Mary Grace Bellotti, the Holy Midwife Who Invoked St. Gerard

Throughout her relatively short life of just forty-five years, Mary Grace Bellotti accomplished great things for the honor and glory of God. She did the ordinary things in life in an extraordinary way. She ministered to and cured the sick, consoled the dying, delivered babies and counseled and encouraged others in their Catholic faith. People had come from far and wide to seek out her help and become the beneficiaries of her God-given gifts of healing and reading of minds and hearts. They called her nurse, healer and "Saint of the Mountain."

Although many benefited from her holiness and good works, God had other plans for her. He decided that he wanted her to come to her true home in heaven. Toward the end of her earthly pilgrimage, she became bedridden and suffered greatly due to a buildup of water pressing against her heart. A priest from St. Michael's Monastery in Union City, New Jersey, visited with her and then later offered a mass for her intentions. After having received the Last Rites of the Church by a Father Ferdinando Anazalone of St. Nicholas Church, she passed on peacefully to meet her Lord and God on November 10, 1927, the Feast of St. Andrew of Avellino.

At first glance, her life, death and funeral look like the scenes out of a movie or documentary. She was waked in her home, which was known as the "Chapel House." It was there in her chapel at 508 Fourth Street in Union City (formerly West Hoboken) that throngs of people came to pay their last respects as they filed past her casket. Four days after her death, on November

14, a Solemn High Mass was offered for
the repose of her soul at St. Michael's
Monastery in Union City, N.J.

As if the crowds of hundreds who
sought her out not only in life but
now also in death were not enough to
convince one of her holiness of life,
something further transpired after the
crowds followed her procession to Third
Calvary Cemetery in Long Island City
in New York. Those in attendance
witnessed something unusual. As her
casket was being lowered into the
ground, a strange woman who had been
crying and praying suddenly stood up
after being in a prostrate position. She then screamed and reported to those
present that she was cured and received a favor through the deceased woman
known as the "Saint of the Mountain."

Mary Grace Belotti, devotee of St.
Gerard. *Courtesy of the archives of Reverend
Thomas D. Nicastro Jr.*

Who is this woman of great faith and holiness of life who labored tirelessly
on behalf of souls for Jesus Christ? During her short span of life, Mary
Grace Bellotti achieved the heights of sanctity and died in God's graces one
day after her forty-fifth birthday. Her cause for canonization was formally
introduced on a diocesan level approximately in 1963. Previously, her cause
was introduced by Reverend Father Andrew Kenny, C.P. (Congregation of
the Passion of Our Lord Jesus Christ or the Passionists) of St. Michael's
Monastery in Union City to Bishop Walsh, bishop of Newark, but nothing
resulted from this. Between the years 1956 and 1958, devotees of Mary
Grace began to form a society in honor of her great patron, St. Gerard
Majella, and in her memory. In the late 1960s, Bishop Martin W. Stanton,
auxiliary bishop of the Archdiocese of Newark, was presented with and
received the official opening of the informative process for Mary Grace's
beatification and canonization.

As I begin to take you on a journey back in time, let me first say that in
telling you the story of Mary Grace's life, if I use the words holy, saint,
saintly, holiness of life or heroic in virtue, I am in no way presupposing the
judgment of the Holy See in the matter of canonizing saints. I humbly submit
these writings to the judgment of the Official Church and its decision. I am
merely reporting what others have testified under oath in an ecclesiastical

court concerning Mary Grace's holiness in striving to live a life of greater perfection in the eyes of God.

The servant of God, Mary Grace Belloti was born on November 9, 1882 in a small Italian village called Laurenzana in the province of Potenza. Accordingly to the baptismal records of the "Mother Church," the Church of the Assumption, Mary Grace was baptized three short days later by Father Rocco Roborlicino. Being the custom of the day, she was confirmed by Monsignor Nicola Gesualdo, of the Archdiocese of Acerenza, two years later on April 27, 1884. She lived with her parents, Joseph and Maria Teresa Marchetta, in an old stone house on the Street of the Seven Towers.

As was the custom with many Italians in the 1880s, Mary Grace's father left Italy for America looking for work so he could support his family. When Joseph left Mary Grace, she was only two years old. For the next seven years, she was raised solely by her mother, Maria Teresa. As she grew older, she desired greatly to see her father whom she had never known. It was about this time in 1891 that she and her mother made a pilgrimage to the Shrine of Our Lady of Mount Viggiano. They made the journey barefoot, fasting and abstaining along with other pilgrims to spiritually prepare themselves for the arrival at the shrine.

Upon arrival, Mary Grace knelt in intense prayer before Our Blessed Lady. During the time before the statue, our lady manifested herself in a vision and told the child, "Your father is preparing to leave America now, and he will come to you. Having received your grace, pray for the crippled boy who is beside you, for he does not know how to pray." After Mary Grace prayed with great faith and devotion, the crippled child was instantaneously cured. He then discarded his crutches and headed straight to his parents, who were nearby. This episode early on in her life is considered to be the first of many cures or graces received through Mary Grace's intercession. Interestingly, there are several parallels in Mary Grace's childhood and that of St. Gerard Maiella, who would later in her adult life become her heavenly patron. For example, as a child, Mary Grace, like St. Gerard, had great devotion to the Blessed Virgin Mary under the title of Our Lady of Mount Carmel. As a child, both Mary Grace and St. Gerard learned the importance of prayer, fasting and abstinence. Very often, she would treasure visits to the Blessed Sacrament over playing with childhood friends. Gerard, too, spent many long hours in prayer before our Divine Lord in the Blessed Sacrament. Of note as well is the fact that both Mary Grace's mother and St. Gerard's mother were instrumental in teaching their precocious children the truths of their holy Catholic faith, such as the catechism and sacred scripture.

APPENDIX I

Although Mary Grace had no formal education, she amazed many who knew her. She quoted sacred scripture. They said her talks were given in the style of a homily. Although St. Gerard received no formal education or training in sacred theology or scripture, he was able to confound the most learned ecclesiastics of his day by expounding on the truths of our holy Catholic faith with such ease and clarity.

As Mary Grace grew, she acquired the skills of cooking and embroidery. Because of her giftedness in both areas, especially the art of cooking, she was asked to cook a special dinner for the bishop when he came to her town to administer the sacrament of Confirmation. She viewed this as doing a special work for God by giving back to him and the Church, through the special abilities she received from him.

It was while praying in church that she met her future husband, Luigi La Perchia, a skilled laborer from Northern Italy (Piedmonti). They got married on December 3, 1903, in the Church of the Assumption in Laurenzana by Father R.C. Sica. Within six months, they departed from the Port of Naples for America seeking a better way of life and arrived in New York's harbor on May 17, 1904. They found their way to the lower east side of Manhattan and lived for a brief period on Thompson Street.

Surely it must have been a harrowing experience to leave Italy for an unknown place. They experienced danger as well while crossing the ocean due to a heavy storm. Now after arriving in a totally new environment and settling in a different type of neighborhood from what they experienced in their small town in Italy, they had to venture out into the unknown. However, as always, Mary Grace prayed with great fervor to the Blessed Mother. Just as the Blessed Mother appeared before her with St. Joseph and the child Jesus and assured her of her safety during this storm at sea, so now they continued to watch over and guide Mary Grace's steps in America.

It was while living on Thompson Street that she made frequent visits to St. Anthony's Church. Soon after their arrival in New York, Mary Grace recognized a change in her husband. He strongly resented her religious practices and devotions. Her piety was an affront to him. In turn, Luigi became a drinker, a gambler and a womanizer. On many occasions over the next several years of their married life, he placed great demands on her to abandon her pious practices, devotions and prayer life. Several times, he became violent and beat her, hoping to convince her to relinquish her holy way of life. She just accepted these terrible outbursts and abuse as her cross in life. She responded by simply fulfilling her duty as a good Christian wife. During her marriage to Luigi, she became pregnant seven times; however, she had four miscarriages and two infant deaths. The only survivor was their first-born child, their daughter Nunziata, known as Nancy, who was born on September 11, 1904.

After spending approximately four years in Manhattan's lower east side, the family decided to move across the Hudson to West Hoboken now Union City, New Jersey. They rented an apartment on Rose Street, now Twenty-first Street, near St. Michael's Monastery. It was there at her beloved St. Michael's that she became involved with teaching little children not only embroidery but also about their holy Catholic faith, especially about the lives of the saints. Within a year, Mary Grace and her husband, Luigi, purchased a house on Summit Avenue. Luigi, however, continued down the wrong path, and our dear Mary Grace paid the price. The abuse continued, and Mary Grace continued to offer her suffering and hardship to Almighty God. It was during these trying times that Mary Grace became friends with two priests from the monastery who spoke Italian though they were not of Italian descent. Eventually, Father Andrew Kenny C.P. and Father Dominic Lagenbacher C.P. became her confessors. Mary Grace was introduced to a saint whose devotion was promoted by the Passionist community (formally known as Congregation of the Passion of Our Lord Jesus Christ) in Union City, that being St. Gemma Galgani. As time passed, our dear Mary Grace achieved great heights in the spiritual life through prayer, fasting and almsgiving. As Mary Grace was progressing in the spiritual realm, her husband increased his promiscuous lifestyle.

The family was on the move again by 1913. They now lived on New York Avenue in Union City. It was there during her prayer time that our Divine Lord came to her and asked her to do some special work for him. This work was to include helping women in childbirth, visiting sick people, more intense prayer and fasting. Gradually, as her apostolate grew, Luigi became increasingly upset with her, and along with that came more beatings and more abuse. As the situation became increasingly worse, Luigi threatened to kill her and put an end to her holy way of life.

It was around this time that Mary Grace took an active interest in those who were to be confirmed. She became a sponsor for many young people who are still living today and remember her as an exceptionally holy individual.

Mary Grace was also actively assisting doctors in delivering babies as a midwife, and her skill became so well known that the doctors nicknamed her "Nurse." Living up to her nickname, she very often cared for the sick and the dying, offering prayers for their recovery and comfort in their hour of need.

APPENDIX I

On October 16, 1913, Mary Grace first encountered St. Gerard Maiella, whose feast was being celebrated at St. Ann's Church in Hoboken, New Jersey. Little did Mary Grace know that on that day, as she walked in procession praying the rosary as the men of the parish carried this great saint on their shoulders, she would forge a very special spiritual bond and friendship with this great man of God. Soon she came to realize that St. Gerard would be the ideal patron for her based on her chosen profession. After choosing him as her patron and heavenly protector, she then very zealously spread devotion to him since he was not yet well known in the United States. Now armed with a powerful heavenly patron, she intensified her spiritual and corporal works of mercy especially for the sick and the dying.

Her daily devotions included prayers not only to her heavenly patron St. Gerard but also to other great saints like St. Anthony, St. Michael the Archangel, St. Joseph, St. Rocco and St. Andrew of Avellino. Added to this was a daily meditation to Christ Crucified and praying the Stations of the Cross. Like her patron, St. Gerard, she often had masses said weekly for the souls in purgatory and fasted on Wednesdays, Fridays and Saturdays.

Mary Grace was to incur the wrath of her irate husband one last time, and again, he threatened to take her life. With this ultimate act of violence, they separated in 1916. Mary Grace and her daughter, Nancy, age eleven, moved to 81 Spring Street (now called Bergenline Avenue.)

In addition to an intense prayer life, visiting the sick and delivering babies as a midwife, Mary Grace contributed generously to the Church and her mission. Donations were sent to the Francisicans, the Holy Cross Order, the Shrine of St. Gerard at Materdomini in Avellino and other places. The stipends or donations were for masses in honor of the saints, for the holy souls in purgatory and special intentions.

After moving to the corner house on Spring Street, she was introduced to Father Peter della Guistina. He was the curate at Our Lady of Mount Carmel in Newark. It was during this period in her life that she forged a spiritual friendship with Father Della Guistina. He assisted her in her apostolate by sending people to see her since he recognized her holiness of life.

As I researched Mary Grace's life, I began to see she was similar in a way to St. Andre Besette of Canada as well. There were differences and many similarities. Yes, Mary Grace was not religious in vows but she was a dedicated lay person, a midwife who consecrated herself to the Lord, the spread of the Gospel and the teachings of the Catholic Church, with a special emphasis on devotion to the saints of God. Like St. Andre Besette of Canada, the sick came to Mary Grace in great numbers. Her reputation, like St. Andre, spread far and wide to the degree that she had to reserve herself to only desperate cases when visiting those who were homebound. Her home had a chapel like St. Andre's chapel, built upon an elevated area. She was known as the "Saint on the Mountain," while still others referred to her as the "Faith Healer." People would come from all over and began gathering at her home as early as 4:00 a.m. Reports of cures and people being led back to the faith began to spread far and wide, as far away as California, New York and Ohio. Because she was gifted with the ability to read peoples' minds and hearts, she knew exactly who needed help the most, as well as who had serious problems to be dealt with.

Her advice was always sound, solid, compassionate and understanding. Most of all, she encouraged them to pray to the Holy Trinity, seek the intercession of Mary and the saints, do penance, go to confession, attend mass, receive holy communion, pray for the Holy Souls in purgatory and live a good, holy life as an example for others to emulate.

It should be noted that Mary Grace never expected payment from anyone or charged a fee for helping those in need. However, whatever freewill offerings were left by the faithful she donated to various churches and helped the poor. She gave to the missions, St. Gerard's Shrine in Materdomini and to Sisters of St. Francis in Bayonne, New Jersey.

Because of the growing crowds of faithful who visited her regularly, she needed larger quarters. On February 1, 1922, a contractor and architect were hired to build a house at 508 Hague Street, which was later changed to Fourth Street (Union City). She named the chapel on Hague Street the House of St. Gerard.

Many of the faithful who received special favors donated statues to the chapel in gratitude. Mary Grace dedicated the altar to St. Joseph. She asked Monsignor Rocco Pellettieri from Mount Viggiano, Italy, to consecrate the altar and offer the first mass. In that same year of 1922, when she had moved the new house on Hague Street, a fire burned most of the block, but the "Chapel House" was spared during that hot summer day in July.

For the next four years, Mary Grace continued her spiritual work and apostolic zeal for Jesus Christ, but health problems gradually slowed her down. During this period of time, her husband, Luigi, whom she had been separated from for almost ten years, had died of carcinoma of the mouth at Memorial Hospital in New York. Very shortly thereafter, she married for a second time to Umberto Cavalli, who admired her and viewed her as a very holy person. He even considered her a saint. In September 1926, she and her new husband decided to move to Palisades Park, New Jersey. She had hoped that the country air would help her with her health problems. Unfortunately, 1029 Bergen Boulevard would not be her home for long, since her health was rapidly declining. Around September or October 1927, she was confined to bed due to water that had accumulated and pressed against her heart. Mary Grace bore her intense pain without complaint and offered up her sufferings for the holy souls in purgatory.

Shortly before her holy death, she was visited by Father Andrea of St. Michael's Monastery. A mass was offered for her health and well-being. Soon thereafter, our dear Mary Grace received the Last Rites of the Church from Father Ferdinando Anzalone, O.M.I. (Oblates of Mary Immaculate) of St. Nicholas Church. She died peacefully on November 10, 1927, making one last offering of her self as a total commitment to God before leaving for her eternal home in heaven.

She was then waked at the Chapel House of St. Gerard, where hundreds of grateful friends and people visited her one last time to say goodbye to the "faith healer" and the "Saint on the Mountain." Bosetti Funeral Home on Bergenline Avenue took care of the arrangements for the funeral. The Solemn High Mass of Christian Burial was offered on November 14, 1927, at St. Michael's Monastery in Union City, New Jersey. The Mass and burial were attended by a very large number of faithful who admired her and looked upon her as a Christian woman who was very close to God, the Blessed Mother and the saints. She was interred at Calvary Cemetery in Long Island City, New York. (Third Calvary, Section 25, Range 8, Plot B, Grave 15.)

Even though more than three quarters of a century have passed, the memory of Mary Grace Bellotti has not dimmed; her memory seems to only increase. Her good works and holiness seem to flourish. Mary Grace's lay apostolate has grown over the years. The lay men and women working for the honor and glory of God and his saints, especially St. Gerard, has evolved into what is now the present-day St. Gerard Maiella Society in Memoriam of Mary Grace Belloti. This society was under the spiritual direction of Father Michael Fuino, the retired pastor of St. Anthony's Church in Union City, where he was pastor from 1963 to 1980.

In 1977, the association supported the Mary Grace Bellotti League of Lay Apostles. In 1980, Father Michael Fuino was named the Postulator of Mary Grace's cause by the former Archbishop of Newark, Most Reverend Peter Leo Gerety.

There was a shrine erected in honor of St. Gerard on November 10, 1984, at St. Mary's Church in Staten Island, New York, by the St. Gerard

"Saint of the Mountain"

Maiella Society in Memoriam of Mary Grace Bellotti. Lastly, in February 1988, an additional office was dedicated by the society in Fort Lauderdale, Florida, to promote the cause of Mary Grace's canonization.

The following are testimonials, printed with permission, given by those who actually knew Mary Grace.

Mrs. Michelina Grace Peluso in one of her letters to Mrs. Geraldine Passariello, spoke of Mary Grace Bellotti in this way. "Mary Grace was a reflection of God's love." Mary Grace died when Michelina was eleven years old; however, Michelina remembers visiting Mary Grace's chapel with her mother. One of Michelina's brothers, Joseph, had asthma. Mary Grace,

Grave of Mary Grace Belotti in New York. *Courtesy of the archives of Reverend Thomas D. Nicastro Jr.*

she said, "rested her hand on his chest and my brother was relieved of his asthma." In a similar vein, there was a young girl present at the chapel in West Hoboken who had been blind. Michelina said that the little girl "was now able to see—through the intercession of St. Gerard and Mary Grace."

Michelina relates the following incident at the end of her letter. "In the year of 1940 my two oldest children and I were visiting at my parents home in North Bergen, New Jersey, a man came to the door, he told us Maria Grazia sent him. We told him she was dead, he said, I know but she sent me—I asked what his name was and all he said was, I know you but you don't know me."

Harry De Risi was around twenty years old when he met Mary Grace. When writing his letter, he was ninety years old and had been praying to Mary Grace for seventy years. He said he received a lot of answers to his prayers and said, "Crowds of people stormed in to see her and were happy when they left." Harry's mother prayed to Mary Grace for her family, all the sick and for family members to die a happy death. He concludes by saying, "I know my favors were granted, twice I was plucked from death…"

In her letter to G. Passariello, Josephine LaViola said "…she blessed and helped many people with St. Gerard's Relic." She continued later on in the letter, "…everyone called her 'healer'. I remember after all these years, I was only 16 or 17 years old when she passed away, that a person was healed at her grave site. We do not have any proof of this, but this is what was said for sometime after her death…"

With this beautiful story of a "holy" layperson and midwife and her devotion to the saints and the Blessed Mother, we see that common ordinary people can do extraordinary things with God's grace for his honor and glory. Maybe you and I can learn from their example and do the same. Clement of Rome, who was a first century bishop, once said, "Follow the Saints, because those who follow them will become Saints."

Novena in Honor of
St. Gerard Maiella, C.Ss.R.

First Day

St. Gerard, ever full of faith, obtain for me that, believing firmly all that the Church of God proposes to my belief, I may strive to secure through a holy life the joys of eternal happiness.

Then say nine Hail Marys, with the following versicle and prayer (repeated on each day of the novena).

V. Pray for us, O Saint Gerard.
R. That we may be made worthy of the promises of Christ.

Let us pray.

O Almighty and everlasting God, who didst draw to thyself Saint Gerard, even from his tenderest years, making him conformable to the Image of Thy Crucified Son, grant we beseech Thee, that imitating his example, we may be made like unto the same Divine Image, through Jesus Christ Our Lord. Amen.

SECOND DAY

St. Gerard, most generous saint, who from thy tenderest years didst care so little for the goods of earth, grant that I may place all my confidence in Jesus Christ alone, my true Treasure, who alone can make me happy in time and in eternity.

THIRD DAY

Saint Gerard, bright seraph of love, who despising all earthly love, didst consecrate thy life to the service of God and thy neighbor, promoting God's glory in thy lowly state, and ever ready to assist the distressed and console the sorrowful, obtain for me, I beseech thee, that loving God the only Good and my neighbor for His sake, I may be hereafter united to Him forever in glory.

FOURTH DAY

Saint Gerard, spotless lily of purity, by thy angelic virtue and thy wonderful innocence of life thou didst receive from the Infant Jesus and His Immaculate Mother, sweet pledges of tenderest love, grant, I beseech thee, that I may ever strive manfully in my life-long fight, and thus win the crown that awaits the brave and the true.

FIFTH DAY

Saint Gerard, model of holy obedience, who through thy life didst heroically submit thy judgment to those who represent Jesus Christ to thee, thus sanctifying thy lowliest actions, obtain for me from God, cheerful submission to His Holy Will and the virtue of perfect obedience, that I may be made conformable to Jesus, my Model, who was obedient even to death.

SIXTH DAY

Saint Gerard, most perfect imitator of Jesus Our Redeemer, do thou whose greatest glory was to be humble and lowly, obtain that I too, knowing my littleness in God's sight, may be found worthy to enter the kingdom that is promised to the humble and lowly of heart.

SEVENTH DAY

Saint Gerard, unconquered hero, most patient in suffering, do thous who didst glory in infirmity, and under slander and most cruel ignominy didst rejoice to suffer with Christ, obtain for me patience and resignation in my sorrows, that I may bravely bear the cross that is to gain for me the crown of everlasting glory.

EIGHTH DAY

Saint Gerard, true lover of Jesus in the Blessed Sacrament of the Altar, do thou who didst kneel long hours before the Tabernacle, and there didst taste the joys of Paradise, obtain for me, I beseech thee, the spirit of prayer and an undying love for the Most Holy Sacrament, that thus receiving frequently the Body and Blood of Jesus, I may daily grow in His holy love and merit the priceless grace of loving Him even to the end.

NINTH DAY

Saint Gerard, most favored child of heaven, to whom Mary gave the Infant Jesus in the day of thy childhood, to whom she sweetly came before thou didst close thine eyes in death, obtain for me I beseech thee, so to seek and love my Blessed Mother during life, that she may be my joy and consolation in this valley of tears, until with thee, before the throne of God, I may praise her goodness for all eternity. Amen.

Occasional Prayers

PRAYER FOR SPECIAL BLESSINGS

Dear St. Gerard, we rejoice in thy happiness and glory; we bless the Lord who endowed thee with the choicest gifts of His grace; we congratulate thee for corresponding so faithful with them. Obtain for us, we pray thee, some part of thy angelic purity, thy burning love for Jesus in the Tabernacle, thy tender devotion to Mary Immaculate. In thy brotherly love, which made thee the support of the poor, the comforter of the afflicted and the apostle of the most forsaken souls, grant me the favors for which I now pray.

(Here, mention them privately.)

O most Powerful Patron, who hast always helped those who prayed to thee, intercede for me before the Throne of God. O Good Saint, to thee I confide my fervent prayers; graciously accept them and before the end of these days of prayer, let me experience in some way the effects of thy powerful intercession. Amen.

PRAYER AGAINST THE FORCES OF ANTI-LIFE

O great Wonderworker of our day, St. Gerard, powerful protector of the mother and her unborn child, beg God, we beseech thee, to crush the mounting forces of anti-life; and to enlighten those who walk in this deadly way that they may see the enormity of their sin and return to the generous observance of the divine law. Pray, too, for mothers that they may prize the great privilege of motherhood and that they may bring up their children in the holy love and fear of God; so saving their own immortal souls and furthering the honor and glory of their Maker; through Christ, Our Lord. Amen

Priest: Pray for us, O Great Saint Gerard!
People: That we may be made worthy of the promises of Christ!
All: O Almighty and Eternal Father, Who, in Thy all-wise Providence, hast deigned to raise up St. Gerard, to be the glorious protector of the mother and her unborn child: grant we beseech Thee, through the powerful intercession of this, Thy servant, that all thee diabolical forces of anti-life may be destroyed from the face of the earth forever: that so the Christian family may once more flourish to the praise and eternal glory of Thy Holy Name. This we ask through the merits of Our Lord and Savior, Jesus Christ, Thy Son, Who liveth and reigneth with Thee and the Holy Ghost- God for ever and ever. Amen.

PRAYER FOR MOTHERHOOD

O good St. Gerard, powerful intercessor before God and Wonderworker of our day, I call upon thee and seek thy aid. Thou who on earth didst always fulfill God's designs, help me to do the holy Will of God. Beseech the Master of Life, from Whom all paternity proceedeth, to render me fruitful in offspring that I may raise up children to God in this life and heirs to the Kingdom of His Glory in the world to come. Amen.

PRAYER FOR A MOTHER WITH CHILD

O Almighty and Everlasting God Who through the operation of the Holy Ghost, didst prepare the body and soul of the glorious Virgin Mary to be a worthy dwelling place of Thy Divine Son; and, through the operation of the same Holy Ghost, didst sanctify St. John the Baptist, while still in his mother's womb; hearken to the prayers of Thy humble servant who implores Thee, through the intercession of St. Gerard, to protect her (me) amid the dangers of child-bearing and to watch over the child with which Thou hast deigned to bless her (me); that it may be cleansed by the saving water of baptism and, after a Christian life on earth, it may with its mother, attain everlasting bliss in Heaven. Amen.

LITANY OF ST. GERARD

Lord, have mercy on us,
Christ, have mercy on us.
Lord, have mercy on us.
Christ, hear us.
Christ, graciously hear us.
God, the Father of Heaven, have mercy on us.
God, the Son, Redeemer of the world, have mercy on us.
God, the Holy Ghost, have mercy on us.
Holy Trinity, one God, have mercy on us.
Holy Mary, Mother of Perpetual Help, pray for us.
St. Joseph, Foster father of Christ, Pray for us.
St. Alphonsus, founder of the Congregation of the Most Holy Redeemer, pray for us.
St. Gerard, endowed with extraordinary graces from early childhood, pray for us.
St. Gerard, perfect type of a faithful servant, pray for us.
St. Gerard, Shining example for the laboring classes, pray for us.
St. Gerard, great lover of prayer and work, pray for us.
St. Gerard, seraphic adorer of the most Blessed Sacrament, pray for us.
St. Gerard, living image of the Crucified Saviour, pray for us.
St. Gerard, most devoted client of the Immaculate Virgin Mary, pray for us.
St. Gerard, bright mirror of innocence and penance, pray for us.
St. Gerard, silent victim of ignominious calumny, pray for us.
St. Gerard, great before God by thy deep humility, pray for us.
St. Gerard, truly wise by thy childlike simplicity, pray for us.
St. Gerard, supernaturally enlightened in divine mysteries, pray for us.
St. Gerard, solely desirous of pleasing God, pray for us.
St. Gerard, zealous promoter of the conversion of sinners, pray for us.

St. Gerard, wise counselor in the choice of vocation, pray for us.
St. Gerard, enlightened guide in the direction of souls, pray for us.
St. Gerard, kind friend of the poor and distressed, pray for us.
St. Gerard, safe refuge in sickness and sorrow, pray for us.
St. Gerard, wonderful protector on unbaptized children, pray for us.
St. Gerard, compassionate intercessor in all our wants, pray for us.
St. Gerard, exalted by God through astonishing miracles, pray for us.
St. Gerard, ornament and glory of Redemptorist Order, pray for us.

Lamb of God, who takest away the sins of the world—Spare us, O Lord.
Lamb of God, who takest away the sins of the world—Graciously hear us, O Lord.
Lamb of God, who takest away the sins of the world—Have mercy on us, O Lord.

V. Pray for us, St. Gerard.
R. That we may be made worthy of the promises of Christ.

Let us pray.

O God, who didst deign to draw St. Gerard unto Thyself from his youth, and to make him conformable to the image of Thy Crucified Son: grant, we beseech Thee, that following his example, we may be transformed into the same image. Through the same Christ, Our Lord.

R. Amen.

Notes

Introduction

1. Reverend O.R. Vassall-Philips, *Life of St. Gerard Majella, Lay Brother of the Congregation of the Most Holy Redeemer* (London: Byans Gates and Washbourne, Ltd., 1923), xxiii.
2. Reverend Charles Dilgskron, C.S.s.R., *Life of Blessed Gerard Majella* (New York: Redemptorist Fathers, 1896), 428.
3. John Carr, C.Ss.R., *To Heaven Through A Window* (New York: Declan X McMullen Company, Inc., 1949), 163.
4. Ibid.
5. Michael Immerso, *Newark's Little Italy: The Vanished First Ward* (Newark, NJ: Rutgers University Press, 1997), 158.

Chapter 1

6. Giovanni Pinto, "L'Italico," *New Jersey* 4, no. 1 (Spring 1977): 11.
7. Ibid.
8. Immerso, *Newark's Little Italy*, pg. 1.
9. Pinto, "L'Italico," 11.
10. Immerso, *Newark's Little Italy*, 65.
11. Gary Genuario, Gerard Nazzareto, and Father Thomas Nicastro, script for documentary, "The One Hundred Year Anniversary of the Feast of St. Gerard Maiella" (New Jersey: S. Sefcik Productions, 1999): 2.
12. Constance Petrucelli Ferrante, *A Walk Through Time: A Symbolic Analysis of the Devotion to St. Gerard Maiella* (New Brunswick, NJ: Rutgers University, 1993), 53.
13. Genuario, et al., "Anniversary of the Feast," 6.
14. Ibid.
15. Immerso, *Newark's Little Italy*, 91.
16. Ibid., 88.

Chapter 2

17. Genuario, et al., "Anniversary of the Feast," 10.
18. Immerso, *Newark's Little Italy*, 67.
19. Pinto, "L'Italico," 4.
20. Immerso, *Newark's Little Italy*, 67.

21. Ibid.
22. Ferrante, *A Walk Through Time*, 54–55.
23. Immerso, *Newark's Little Italy*, 82.
24. Mary DePiano Goldstein, "Centennial Celebration Book: St. Lucy's Parish History," 1991.

Chapter 3

25. Immerso, *Newark's Little Italy*, 140.
26. Ibid., 141.
27. Ibid.
28. Goldstein, "Centennial Celebration Book."
29. Ibid.
30. Ibid.
31. Ibid.
32. Ibid.
33. Immerso, *Newark's Little Italy*, 69.
34. Goldstein, "Centennial Celebration Book."

Chapter 4

35. Monsignor Joseph Granato, interview in documentary script, "The One Hundred Year Anniversary of the Feast of St. Gerard" (New Jersey, Sefcik Production, 1999): 18–19.
36. Genuario, et al., "Anniversary of the Feast," 30.
37. Immerso, *Newark's Little Italy*, 156.

Chapter 5

38. Congressional Record, Proceedings and Debate of the Ninety-fifth Congress, First Session, vol. 123, no. 165.
39. Goldstein, "Centennial Celebration Book."
40. Genuario, et al., "Anniversary of the Feast," 23.
41. Immerso, *Newark's Little Italy*, 157.
42. Genuario, et al., "Anniversary of the Feast," 23.
43. William Gordon, "Blessed Event: Feast of St. Gerard Reunites Newark's Italian-Americans" *Newark Star Ledger*, October 14, 1997.
44. Ferrante, *A Walk Through Time*, 224–25.
45. Mary Ann Castronovo Fusco, "How a Church Brings Life to Newark's Little Italy," *New York Times*, October 10, 1999.
46. Ibid.
47. Ferrante, *A Walk Through Time*, 53–54.
48. Ibid., 53.
49. Ibid., 55.
50. Ibid., 56.

NOTES

51. Michael Immerso, "Nevarca, A Celebration of the Italian American Experience in Newark", October–December 1999. A cooperative project of the Newark Public Library; Rutgers University's Institute on Ethnicity, Culture and the Modern Experience; the Joseph M. and Geraldine C. LaMotta Chair in Italian Studies at Seton Hall University; New Jersey Performing Arts Center; the Newark Museum, the North Ward Center, Inc.; New Jersey Historical Society Italian Vice Consulate; Columbus Hospital; the Center for Italian and Italian American Culture; Newark Preservation and Landmarks Committee; the office of the mayor; Newark Municipal Council; Archdiocese of Newark; St. Lucy's Roman Catholic Church; and the *Italian Tribune*.
52. Ibid.
53. Ibid.

Chapter 6

54. Reverend Edward St. Omer, C.S.s.R., *The Wonder Worker of Our Days: Life, Virtue and Miracles of St. Gerard Majella, Lay Brother of the Congregation of the Most Holy Redeemer* (Boston: Mission Church Press, 1907), 225.
55. Ibid., 251.
56. Peter Heinegg, *St Gerard Majella, His Writings and Spirituality*, Angelomichele de Spirito, "Saint Gerard and the Popular Piety of His Time", (Liguori, MO: Liguori Publications, 2000–2002), 63.
57. Peter Heinegg, *St. Gerard Majella, His Writings and Spirituality*, Gabriele DeRosa, "The Penitential Piety of Gerard Majella" (Liguori, Missouri, Liguori Publications, 2000-2002), 83.
58. Carr, *To Heaven Through A Window*, 289.
59. Ibid., 291.
60. Immerso, *Newark's Little Italy*, 158.

Bibliography

Adels, Jill Haak. *The Wisdom of the Saints*. New York: Oxford University Press, 1987.

Attwater, Donald. *A Dictionary of Saints*. Great Britain: Hazell Watson & Viney Ltd., 1965.

Benedetti, Claudio, C.Ss.R. *St. Gerardo Maiella*. Materdomini, Italy: Tipagrafia, S. Gerardo Maiella, 1929.

Bonomo, Umberto, C.Ss.R. *I Nostri Santi*. New York: Vatican City Religious Book Co. Inc., 1946.

Brother Ernest, CSC. *He's a Man: A Story of St. Gerard Majella*. Notre Dame, IN: Dujane Press, 1956.

Capone, Domenico, (a cura di). *Le Lettere di S. Gerardo Maiella* (Contributi Gerardini, 1) Valsele Tipografica, Materdomini (AV) 1980, 382 p. (coll. S. Majorano).

Carr, John, C.Ss.R. *Saint Gerard Majella*. Westminster, MD: Newman Press, 1959.

———. *To Heaven Through a Window: The Life of St. Gerard Majella*. New York: McMullen Books, Inc., 1949.

Cevetello, Reverend Joseph, F.X. *Crucified with Christ, the Life of Saint Gerard Majella, The Mother's Saint*. New Jersey: self-published, 1979.

Cruz, Joan Carrol. *Mysteries Marvels Miracles in the Lives of the Saints*. Rockford, IL: Tan Books and Publishers, Inc., 1997.

Delaney, John J. *Dictionary of Saints*. New York: Doubleday and Company, Inc., 1980.

Dilgskron, Reverend Charles, C.Ss.R. *Life of Blessed Gerard Majella: Lay Brother of the Congregation of the Most Holy Redeemer*. New York: Redemptorist Fathers, 1896.

Dolan, Jay P. *The American Catholic Experience*. New York: Image Books, 1985.

Felici, Icilio. *Sott'acqua e Sottovento S. Gerardo Maiella*. Materdomini, Italy: Casa Editrice "S. Gerardo Maiella", 1959.

Ferrante, Constance Petrucelli. *A Walk Through Time: A Symbolic Analysis of the Devotion to St. Gerard Maiella*. New Jersey: 1993.

Ferrante, Nicola. *Storia Meravigliosa Di S. Gerardo Maiella*. Roma, Italy: Coletti Editore Roma, 1965.

Freze, Michael, S.F.O. *The Making of Saints*. Indiana: Our Sunday Visitor Publishing Division, 1991.

Galvin, James J., C.Ss.R. *S. Gerardo Maiella*. Materdomini, Italy: Casa Editrice "S. Gerardo Maiella", 1981.

———. *The Story of St. Gerard Majella, C.Ss.R.* New York: St. Gerard Guild, 1981.

Gregorio, Oreste. *I Ricordi di S. Gerardo a Materdomini*. Materdomini, Italy: Casa Editrice "S. Gerardo Maiella," 1972.

Guardini, Romano. *The Saints in Daily Christian Life*. New York: Dimension Books, 1966.

Helms, Hal M. *Saints Alive*. Orleans, MA: Paraclete Press, 1985.

Immerso, Michael. *Newark's Little Italy: The Vanished First Ward*. Newark, NJ: Rutgers University Press, 1997.

Johnston, Francis W. *The Voice of the Saints*. Rockford, IL: Tan Books and Publishers, Inc., 1986.

Kleinz, Monsignor John P. *The Who's Who of Heaven: Saints for All Seasons*. Westminster, MD: Christian Classics, 1989.

Low, Joseph, Raymond Telleria, Orestes Gregorio and Andrew Sampers. *Spicilegium Historicum Congregationis S Smi Redemptoris*. Rome, Italy: Redemptorist Stories Publication, Annus VIII Fasc. 1960.

Luce, Clare Boothe. *Saints for Now*. San Francisco: Ignatius Press, 1993.

McGreevy, Michael, C.Ss.R. *Gerard Majella, The Mothers Saint*. Liguori, MO: Liguori Publications, 1994.

Molinari, Paul, S.J. *Saints: Their Place in the Church*. New York: Sheed and Ward, 1965.

Moran, J. Anthony. *Pilgrims Guide to America*. Huntington, IN: Our Sunday Visitor Publishing Division, 1992.

Pilla, Eugenio. *S. Gerardo Maiella*. Bari, Italy: Edizioni Paoline, 1966.

Rey-Mermet, Théodule *S. Gerardo, il Fraticello Che Giocava con Dio*. Materdomini, Italy: Casa Editrice "S. Gerardo Maiella," 1977.

Saint-Omer, Reverend Edward, C.Ss.R. The Wonder Worker of Our Days, Life, Virtues, And Miracles of St. Gerard Majella. Boston: Mission Church Press, 1907.

Santoli, Francesco, C.Ss.R. *S. Gerardo Maiella Redentorista*. 1980.

Schiavo, Giovanni. *Italian-American History*, Vol. II. *The Italian Contribution to the Catholic Church in America*. New York: Vigo Press, 1949.

St. Lucy's Church Centennial Celebration 1891–1991. New Jersey: 1991.

Tannoia, Antonio Maria. *The Lives of the Companions of St. Alphonsus*. London: Richardson and son, 1849.

Thurston, Herbert, S.J., and Donald Attwater. *Butler's Lives of The Saints*, Vol. 4. New York: P.J. Kennedy & Sons, 1956.

United States Catholic Conference. *Catholic Shrines and Places of Pilgrimage in the United States*. Washington, D.C.: United States Catholic Conference, 1994.

Vassall-Phillips, Reverend O.R. *Life of Saint Gerard Majella: Lay Brother of the Congregation of the Most Holy Redeemer*. London: Burns, Oates and Washbourne, Ltd., 1923.

Newspapers

Italian Tribune News
Newark Advertiser
Newark Evening News
Newark Evening Star
Newark Star Ledger

About the Author

Reverend Thomas D. Nicastro Jr. was born on February 8, 1961, in Newark. He is the son of Phyllis and the late Gaetano "Tom" Nicastro and the brother of Lisa and Domenick Nicastro. Raised in Newark, he was a parishioner of St. Francis Xavier Church and graduated from St. Francis Xavier grammar school in June 1975. Upon graduation, he attended Essex Catholic High School in Newark and graduated in 1979 with honors in religion.

Desiring to pursue a priestly vocation, he attended Seton Hall University and the College of Seminary of the Immaculate Conception from 1979 to 1983. In the fall of 1984, he received a bachelor of arts degree in modern languages. Father Tom completed his theological studies for the Roman Catholic priesthood on May 22, 1989, receiving a master of divinity degree in pastoral ministry from Immaculate Conception Seminary in South Orange, New Jersey.

He was ordained a deacon on December 8, 1989, on the Solemnity of the Immaculate Conception at St. Augustine Cathedral in Bridgeport, Connecticut, by the then Most Reverend Edward M. Egan, J.C.D., bishop of Bridgeport. He was ordained to the sacred priesthood on May 26, 1990, for service in the Bridgeport Diocese, by Bishop Edward M. Egan, now Edward Cardinal Egan, Archbishop Emeritus of the Archdiocese of New York. He served in various parishes in the Diocese of Bridgeport.

Prior to returning home to New Jersey on October 1, 2003, he also served as assistant master of ceremonies to the then Bishop Egan. He was elected by his priestly peers to serve on the Presbyterial Council before being released for priestly service in the Archdiocese of Newark, the archdiocese he grew up in.

On October 1, 2003, Bishop William E. Lori, S.T.D. formally released Father Nicastro to serve in the Archdiocese of Newark. On June 6, 2008, he was incardinated into the Archdiocese of Newark by Archbishop John J. Myers, D.D., J.C.D. He has since served in various parishes in the archdiocese.

In February 2011, he was appointed parochial vicar of St. Mary's Church in Nutley, New Jersey, where he presently serves.

Prior to his priestly ordination, he was a member of the committee for the Feast of St. Gerard at St. Lucy's Church, Newark, the National Shrine of St. Gerard in America. In conjunction with the feast, he was member and trustee of the St. Gerard Men's Society.

Left: Father Tom Nicastro with Reverend Domenico Barillá, former rector of the International Shrine of St. Gerard. This was the last visit they had before Father Barillá died. *Courtesy of the archives of Reverend Thomas D. Nicastro Jr.*

Below: Father Tom Nicastro preaching at one of the St. Gerard Masses at St. Lucy's Church. *Courtesy of the archives of Mr. Dennis Genuario*

ABOUT THE AUTHOR

In the area of service organizations in the Italian American community, he was a member of the West Essex Chapter of UNICO National prior to moving to Connecticut. In 1989, he was chosen as West Essex UNICO's Man of the Year. While in Stamford, Connecticut, he served as chaplain to the Stamford Chapter of UNICO National. He is the past chaplain of the Belleville Police Department in Belleville, New Jersey. He is presently a member of the Nutley/Belleville Columbus Day Parade Committee.

In November 2009, he received the Man of the Year Award from the Federation of Italian American Societies of New Jersey. On October 8, 2010, he received the Italian Lifetime Heritage Award from the Nutley/Belleville Columbus Parade Committee.

On September 27, 2011, he was installed as chaplain of the St. Mary's Council Knights of Columbus. Presently he is chaplain of the New Jersey State Opera and on February 1, 2012 he was appointed chaplain of the Nutley P.B.A, Nutley Police Department. He is also the chaplain of the following other organizations: West Essex Chapter of UNICO National, the Federation of Italian American Societies of New Jersey and the St. Gerard Men's Society and Ladies' Guild associated with St. Lucy's Church.

Father Tom Nicastro is a lifelong devotee of St. Gerard, a devotion that has been in his family for over 150 years. Annually, he celebrates a Mass in honor of St. Gerard, and for the past several years, he has given the annual novena to St. Gerard at the National Shrine at St. Lucy's Church, Newark, N.J.

At present, he is in the process of completing a book on the life of St. Gerard. In 1999, in preparation for the 100th anniversary of the Feast of St. Gerard, he wrote the original story line and worked on the screenplay for the video "A Walk Through Time" documenting the one hundred years of the Feast of St. Gerard, now available on DVD.

Prior to his death, Revered Domenico Barillá, the former Rector of the International Shrine of St. Gerard Maiella in Materdomini, asked Father Tom to be the official delegate of the International Shrine to the United States. On October 30, 1999, on the occasion of the 100th anniversary of the Feast of St. Gerard, Father Tom was asked to be one of the guest speakers at a symposium at Seton Hall University on the topic of "An Italian Saint and his Community: St. Gerard Maiella and Newark's 'Old First Ward.'" More recently, he was asked to be one of the guest speakers at another symposium on Saturday, May 3, 2008, at the mezzanine on Broad Street in Newark. The topic of the day was "Newark's Little Italy: A Community's Love Story with a City and the Urban Planning Policy Failures that Led to Its Demise." Father Tom spoke specifically on "The Role of the Community's Devotion to St. Gerard in its Survival."

For the last several years, he has dedicated himself to a project dear to his heart: the placement of St. Gerard on the General Roman Calendar and the Liturgical Calendar in the United States and the request to have Rome declare him the official patron saint of mothers, their children and the unborn. The preservation and legacy of the Feast of St. Gerard Maiella at the National Shrine at St. Lucy's Church in Newark remains dear to his heart.

Visit us at
www.historypress.net

www.ingramcontent.com/pod-product-compliance
Lightning Source LLC
Chambersburg PA
CBHW070926150426
42812CB00049B/1516